POLICE STAFF

Quality
Assurance
in Training and
Education

Quality *Assurance* in Training and Education

How to Apply BS5750 (ISO 9000) Standards

Richard Freeman

London • Philadelphia

First published in 1993

Apart from any fair dealing for the purposes of research or private study,
or criticism or review, as permitted under the Copyright, Designs and
Patents Act, 1988, this publication may only be reproduced, stored or
transmitted, in any form or by any means, with the prior permission in
writing of the publishers, or in the case of reprographic reproduction in
accordance with the terms of licences issued by the Copyright Licensing
Agency. Enquiries concerning reproduction outside those terms should
be sent to the publishers at the undermentioned address:

Kogan Page Limited
120 Pentonville Road
London N1 9JN

©Richard Freeman, 1993
The author asserts his moral right under section 77 of the Copyright,
Designs and Patents Act, 1988 to be identified as the author of this
book.

British Library Cataloguing in Publication Data
A CIP record for this book is available from the British Library.

ISBN 0 7494 0868 5

Typeset by Witwell Ltd, Southport
Printed and bound in Great Britain by
Biddles Ltd, Guildford and King's Lynn

Contents

CONTENTS

Introduction

The coming of the market

Worldwide, most training and education institutions have served their locality. Usually their funds have also come from local or national public funds. All that is changing. First, we have seen the development of global training and education markets whether through students travelling thousands of miles to take an MBA course, or through the use of a satellite link to join student and tutor across half the world. Second, we have seen the decreasing role of public funds as governments, both East and West, push once public organizations to seek other sources of money. Training and education are becoming market-orientated.

Once competition enters a market, the providers have to find ways to distinguish their service from that of their competitors. They look for competitive advantage. Some will seek that edge through providing specialist courses or facilities, others through the flexibility of their programmes and yet others through price cutting. For most, though, they will have no option but to compete on quality.

While all providers doubtless like to think of themselves as providing a quality service, any provider who complacently assumes that quality will look after itself will rapidly be overtaken by those who listen to the market. Only those providers who consciously strive to meet the demands of their markets will survive. But what does strive mean? What it does not mean is expecting to be rewarded for hard work. The market rewards results, not effort. So, clearly, striving for quality means working in some way which more effectively delivers results.

The role of quality assurance

The approach that manufacturing industry has taken to achieve the quality edge is quality assurance. Increasingly, training and education organizations are looking to use the same route to deliver markets to them. Quality assurance is a systematic approach to identifying market needs and honing working methods to meet those needs. Organizations can develop and run their own quality assurance schemes but many prefer to adopt a recognized standard and to seek external approval for their system. In the UK, BS 5750 is the standard for quality assurance systems. Internationally, BS 5750 is known as ISO 9000. The two standards are identical in all but name. Thus the standards, methods and advice in this book apply worldwide. For convenience, I have used the term BS 5750 throughout this book. Non-UK readers should read this as ISO 9000, the international standard.

Many training and education organizations have begun to explore how they could adopt this standard; a few have attained the coveted BSI 'kite-mark'. The main reason why so few organizations have achieved the 'kite-mark' is the fact that BS 5750 was designed for manufacturing industry. Its language and approach are alien to training and education. However, its underlying principles, concentrating, as they do, on meeting customer needs, are ones which are fully applicable in the new training and education markets. Somehow, then, we need to find a way of applying BS 5750 to training and education. This book sets out some guidelines on how to apply BS 5750 to training and education.

The book's main aim is to show how the BS 5750 standard can be adapted for the benefit of teachers and learners and without compromising the professional standards which teachers have developed over many years. Too many of the consultants on BS 5750 whose background is in industry are inadvertently persuading trainers and educators to apply the standard in a manner which is detrimental to good teaching, and hence to learners. I hope that the approach which I have adopted in this book will be seen by trainers and teachers as one which allows them to exercise their skills to even better effect than before.

Are training and education different?

I do not intend here to reopen the debate as to where the dividing line is between training and education. What I do intend to do is to comment on the extent to which one book can cover quality assurance in both training and education.

BS 5750, as you will see as we get into the detail, is a single system originally designed to cover all manufacturing, later extended to the service industries, and now being used in training and education. While the strains of this stretching of BS 5750 show all too clearly, it remains a very general set of principles about good management. As such, the principles are highly relevant to both training and education. On the other hand, the application of those principles to the teaching/learning process is often difficult. For example, the product of teaching is both the quality of what the learner experiences (the teaching) and the outcome (what has been learnt). It is easy to monitor the outcome, but very difficult for a QA system to monitor the process. These difficulties, though, are exactly the same in training and education. This book should therefore be equally relevant to each sector and, in writing it, I have only on very few occasions felt it necessary to suggest that either sector will need to plan differently from the other.

11

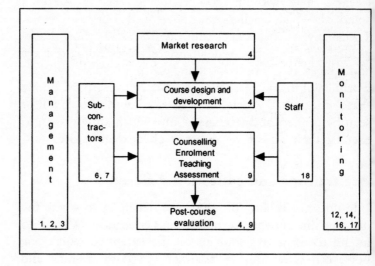

Figure 1 *How BS 5750 relates to the teaching process*

Getting a feel for BS 5750

The 20 separate standards in BS 5750 are not, on the surface, easy to relate to training and education. Indeed some of the 20 standards have almost no application in teaching and learning. In Figure 1, I have selected those of the 20 standards that are highly relevant to the teaching process and tried to relate them to a simple model of presenting a course. As you get further into the book, and especially into Chapter 3, you will probably find it useful to return to this figure from time to time.

Key

The numbers in Figure 1 refer to sub-sections of Section 4

of BS 5750 Part 1. Only the section numbers of major importance to training and education are given here.

1 Management responsibility
2 Quality system
3 Contract review
4 Design control
6 Purchasing
7 Purchaser supplied product

9 Process control
13 Control of non-conforming product
14 Corrective action
16 Quality records
17 Internal quality audits
18 Training

Chapter 1

Principles of Quality Assurance Systems

Quality assurance: a management system

The words 'quality assurance' (QA) have a wonderful mystique about them, giving the impression of a complex set of skills which few of us will ever acquire. No doubt the early developers of QA kept themselves in business through continuing to foster that image. At the risk of having to terminate this book now, the truth is that QA is a grandiose term for any well-run management system. This means that QA is not esoteric, or complex, or beyond the reach of non-specialists. If it were, what would be the point of it? Any QA system which is going to work has to be simple, fitting comfortably alongside – or even inside – everyday working practice.

Why do we want QA?

You may work in a perfect organization where everybody always knows what they are doing, nothing ever arrives late, work is always passed to you in the exact form you need it in, your suppliers never let you down . . . You may, but I doubt it.

For most of us, our experience of work is more frustrating. We can readily recall work which arrived late, work

14

which was so poorly done that it had to be repeated, changes to systems and procedures which we were never told about. In short, most of us, most of the time, think that our organizations could be run more efficiently. QA is an approach that shares that belief.

You can very easily work out whether your organization could benefit from a QA system by considering whether you have ever experienced any of the following:

- work dumped on you which you did not think was your responsibility;
- other people not completing tasks on which your work depended;
- poor quality work performed by others;
- unclear or confusing aims and expectations among your colleagues.

Now look back at your list and ask whether any (or even most) of the problems would not have occurred if:

- people had kept to agreed ways of working;
- work passed to you had met expected formats and quality guidelines;
- you and your colleagues had always been clear as to who did what;
- systems had been in place to detect and correct the problems which occurred.

If you found yourself seeing the second list as an answer to the first, then your organization needs a QA system.

In essence, QA is an approach to organizing work which ensures that:

- the organization's mission and aims are clear and known to all;
- the systems through which work will be done are well thought out, foolproof (well, almost) and communicated to everyone;
- it is always clear who is responsible for what;

15

- what the organization regards as 'quality' is well-defined and documented;
- there are systems to check that everything is working to plan;
- when things go wrong – and they will – there are agreed ways of putting them right.

To see how this approach works in practice, I need to consider a number of possible approaches to documenting and running management systems. I will divide the approaches into undocumented, documented and QA.

Undocumented

In the undocumented approach, the only way to find out how something is done is to ask someone. 'Ask Joe, he always knows', 'Try Mary, I think she's done that before'. In very small organizations, this can work well, but as organizations grow, this 'system' falls apart. Different people do things differently. Two different admissions' tutors apply differing admissions criteria. Two trainers find that they have both booked the same room through two conflicting systems. Essentially, the undocumented system is not a system at all. It's a *laissez-faire* approach in which the organization never decides how anything is to be done.

Documented

Most undocumented systems are intensely frustrating and unproductive. Soon, task by task, methods develop for how things should be done. A booking system here, a marking scheme there . . . but do people keep to these methods? Perhaps. And perhaps not. How would anyone ever know? That is one of the problems with documented systems. It is one thing to set down on paper how tasks should be carried out, but quite another to ensure that those intentions become practice.

Additionally, even if a documented system is fairly well

16

observed in practice, it still lacks any means of reviewing and improving itself. QA overcomes that.

QA

The QA approach to management is very similar to the documented method but it adds three essential extras. These are:

- a method of checking up on how well the system is being adhered to;
- a method of correcting mistakes;
- a method of changing the system if it has become out of date.

This error-correcting aspect of QA is very important. Mistakes and failures will occur. QA honestly recognizes that possibility and prepares for it.

Errors can be of two types:

- human error;
- the agreed method is obsolete.

QA carefully distinguishes between these two cases. In the former case, the error or omission is corrected; in the latter, the method is amended. QA is therefore both a self-correcting and a learning system. It changes to reflect changing needs.

Quality control

Before I move on to a more detailed look at the characteristics of QA, I need to distinguish between QA and quality control.

Quality control is a much more widely known term than QA but the distinction between the two is not always well drawn. Quality control is essentially a method for inspecting for, and rejecting, defective work (although some of its statistical methods can be used to prevent defective work occurring). In training and education, a quality control system might measure exam or test passes and then sack the trainers or teachers who fail to achieve defined pass rates. In such an approach, there is no concept of preventing the problem in the first place. QA is essentially *preventive*, as the word assurance implies. In slogan terms, QA means 'right first time'. It means preventing errors, not putting them right time after time.

Making a start

This section is an overview of the heart of the process of setting up a QA system. It looks at the three basic building blocks which you will need to create:

- your mission;
- your methods;
- your standards.

Your mission

QA starts with a clear sense of what your organization exists to achieve: its mission. This is a time-free, qualitative, statement such as:

- to be the best provider of qualification courses in our area;
- to maintain the highest possible level of repeat business in our area;
- to have a reputation for excellence among parents in our area.

In a well-established college or training centre, it may seem unnecessary to document the mission. 'We all know what we do here', 'It's obvious what this place is for'. Yes . . . but so often different people have different ideas of what the organization is for and of where it is trying to go. If two people go off on holiday, sharing the driving, but each navigating to a different destination, where will they end

18

up? The same question can be asked of any organization which fails to agree to its mission and trusts to an intuitive group view of what it is there for. It is pointless installing a QA system in an organization which has no shared view of what will constitute success.

The mission statement is aspirational. It raises the sights of the organization to a higher level of achievement. The statement is not, however, a set of goals or objectives and in itself a mission statement can never be notched up as 'achieved'. Your organization might have targets for this year such as 'to train 100 learners to NVQ level 3' or 'to gain 70 per cent grade A GCE 'A' level passes'. These can be achieved and once achieved they are in the past. A mission is never achieved in that sense: it is always there challenging you to achieve. (That does not mean that a mission cannot be changed. It can and should change as the external world changes. QA systems include formal methods for reviewing an organization's mission.)

In summary then, a mission statement is:

- a statement of what the organization is there to achieve;
- aspirational;
- in itself a quality statement;
- not a set of objectives or targets.

Methods

Once the mission is agreed, QA systems compel the organization to agree the methods by which things are to be done.

It is usually fairly clear what tasks need to be done in an organization – enrol learners, order books, train, clean teaching rooms – although in new organizations even the list of tasks may be unclear. In more mature organizations, despite superficial order, there may be strongly conflicting views about how each task should be done and, especially, about who should do it. 'No one told me I had to use a marking scheme. I've always done it my own way.'

Problem	Result
What: Tasks are ill-defined	• key tasks not done • tasks get done twice or more than twice
How: Methods are not defined	An individual's methods may: • conflict with the methods of others • confuse people • disrupt systems • result in failure to complete the task
Who: People are not defined	• two people may attempt the same task • a task is left undone

Table 1.1 *Ill-defined working methods cause problems*

Essentially the problems come down to a lack of agreement on:

• what needs to be done – what;
• the method of doing it – how;
• who should do it – who.

Table 1.1 gives some examples of the problems that can follow through 'what, how or who' being ill-defined. If the 'what' is ill-defined, tasks may not get done at all; if the 'how' is ill-defined, different trainers may pursue conflicting methods; and if the 'who' is ill-defined, there is a danger that tasks will lie undone because no one saw them as their responsibility.

Interfaces

There is an additional concept in QA which needs to be introduced here: the interface. Awful as the word is, because it is in common use in QA, I will stick to it. What

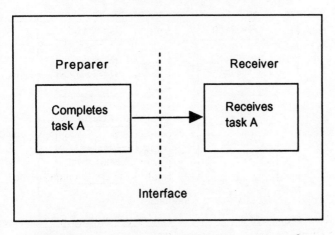

Figure 1.1 *An interface between two people*

QA theory says is that the critical point at which quality can effectively be assured is at the interface between two functions: when person A hands a job over to person B. For example, these are all interfaces:

- an editor hands over a prospectus to a printer;
- an administrator hands a trainer a list of learners for a course;
- a learner hands in an assignment for assessment.

An interface involves a preparer, a receiver and a task, as is illustrated in Figure 1.1. The receiver expects to carry out a particular stage of a process (eg teach a group of learners). He/she can only do this if someone else first enrols the learners. As you will repeatedly see in QA, the idea that handovers at interfaces should be properly done is obvious. QA is often about making sure that the obvious happens.

Some examples for education and training are shown in Figure 1.2. These show how routine activities such as preparing to teach a group or preparing to mark an assignment depend on some prior work being carried out by someone else. The lecturer cannot teach the group without a list of who is to be in the group. Nor can a lecturer mark an assignment which has not been completed.

21

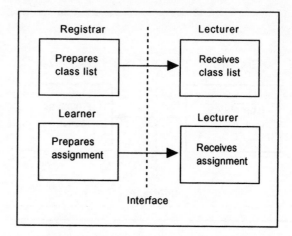

Figure 1.2 *Examples of interfaces*

All this looks a bit abstract until we consider what we all expect to happen at an interface. The receiver expects that the preparer has done his/her job completely and in the agreed manner. Why? Because the receiver cannot do his/ her job unless the preparer has done the same. Given that this handover of work from preparer to receiver is so critical to doing a good job, the interface is often called a *critical interface*. Find all the critical interfaces in your organization, fix them, and you virtually have a QA system. (In modern management jargon, the receiver is often called an *internal customer* and the preparer an *internal supplier*. I have not used these terms since there is fairly widespread dislike of them among trainers and educators.)

In practice, we are all both preparers and receivers as Figure 1.3 shows. Few tasks are initiated in isolation by a tutor or trainer. Most involve carrying out the next stage in a sequence of processes.

Standards

I have said that the receiver expects that the task will be handed over in a completed state and in the agreed form.

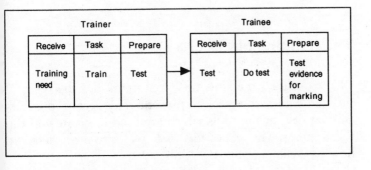

Figure 1.3 *Each preparer is also a receiver*

No tutor is going to mark half an assignment scribbled illegibly on a dozen old envelopes. So QA systems assume that there are agreed standards and/or formats in which tasks are handed over. For the class list, the trainer and administrator might agree that:

- the list is complete;
- names, ages, sexes are accurate;
- the list is typed on A4 paper.

Agreeing these standards is a critical part of setting up a QA system. The process can often prove controversial since opinions differ on how well tasks need to be done. One person might insist that all handouts are typeset, another might think that typewritten – or even handwritten – will do. These problems are easily resolved if there is a general agreement to use the commonest definition of quality: 'fitness for purpose'. This means ensuring that all debates on quality are tested against the customers' expectations. The professional view of the trainer or lecturer bows to what the purchaser is willing to pay for. (It must be admitted, however, that in training and education, there is often room for dispute about who the customer is: is it the learner or the employer who pays the learner's fee?)

The building blocks of a QA system

I have outlined the aims of QA systems and the types of problem which they seek to prevent. This section provides an overview of the tools which are used to create and run QA systems. The rest of the book goes into more detail on how to create and use the tools.

Quality policy

A key part of setting up a quality system is defining a quality policy. The document has to be in a form which all staff can use and understand. To be effective, it has to be clear and specific. For example, it is no use saying, 'We believe that we should always complete everything to the highest possible standards'. Worthy as such a statement is, it is useless as a day-to-day guide on how to get the job done. Instead the policy document might say, 'There will be defined procedures for our ten key functions of: enrolling learners, counselling, assessment, . . .' In outline, a quality policy might cover:

- who is responsible for setting up and running the QA system;
- how the system is to be monitored and reviewed by management;
- for which functions/tasks defined procedures will be written;
- how the implementation of those procedures will be monitored;
- how failures to adhere to the procedures will be corrected.

24

Procedures

I have just started using the term *procedure* and must now explain its special meaning in QA systems.

Not everything that an organization does can be subject to the full rigour of a QA system. To attempt to do so would be overwhelmingly time-consuming. More practically, an organization identifies the functions or tasks where performance *critically affects* the service *as perceived by the users*. (In practice, BS 5750 compels you to cover certain tasks – these will be explained in Chapter 3). Meanwhile, your organization might decide that its critical functions are:

• enrolment and counselling;
• curriculum planning;
• assessment;
• learning resources;
• work experience;
• selection and appointment of staff;
• staff development.

You would then write procedures for each of these. A procedure is a clear and systematic method of setting out how a function is to be carried out and who is responsible for each part of it. A sample procedure appears in Appendix 1 but the full detail of how to design procedures appears in Chapter 4.

Work instructions

For procedures to be easily understood and followed, they must be short and must avoid unnecessary detail. Sometimes more detail is needed to ensure that a job is done in a precise manner. Where this is the case, the extra detail is put into a work instruction. For example, a procedure might contain the paragraph:

25

Mini-buses for trips shall be ordered by the trip organizer at least seven days prior to any trip, using Form ABC99.

Form ABC99 then becomes the work instruction which tells the organizer exactly what details are needed and by whom.

The distinction between procedures and work instructions is ill-defined but essentially is summarized by:

Procedures

* refer to a process that includes many sub-tasks;
* outline what needs to be done.

Work instructions

* refer to just one task;
* provide detailed guidance on how to complete the task.

An example of a work instruction appears in Appendix 2. The details of how to design a work instruction will be discussed in Chapter 5.

Auditing

The quality policy and the procedures can be as good as you like without providing any guarantee that they are being followed. Auditing is the means by which the organization checks that the procedures are really being implemented. Regular checks (audits) are made in a particular and systematic manner (explained in more detail in Chapter 6) to identify whether or not the procedures are being adhered to. Inevitably this involves the potentially threatening process of interviewing the people doing the work. They can easily assume that they are being inspected, which is not the case at all. This impression has to be regularly dispelled by reminding everyone involved that it is the procedure which is being audited, not the person.

Corrective action

Even auditing is not enough to ensure that a QA system works. What happens if the auditing shows that some aspect of a procedure is being ignored? For example, suppose a procedure specifies that each trainer is to receive three copies of any change to the content of a training event before each event starts. Auditing reveals that (a) trainers receive only one copy and (b) the copies arrive a day before the training event starts. The next step is corrective action, i.e. putting right what has been overlooked or done incorrectly. This can result in one of two actions.

- In some cases, the auditing simply reveals that the procedure is out of date. Perhaps the trainers no longer want three copies of the changes. In this case, the action is to amend the procedure.
- In other cases, the procedure is still agreed to be the right way of doing things so the parties involved in the audit have to agree on how best to put things right. If it is too late to correct the past action then attention focuses on preventing the problem from recurring.

Management review

The final part of a QA system is the management review. A committee of senior management holds regular review meetings to assess how well the QA system is meeting the organization's and the customers' needs and how well the system is being run. Such a review would receive summary reports on the system which might document areas such as:

- adherence to the audit schedule – are audits being done on time?
- implementation of corrective action – are problems revealed by audits being put right in the agreed manner and promptly?

27

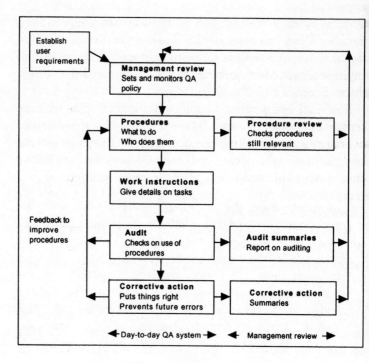

Figure 1.4 *The basic QA system*

- procedure review – are procedures being regularly reviewed by their users and amended if needed?
- mission – is the mission statement still appropriate?

The overall QA approach is a self-regulatory, self-improving one, as is illustrated in Figure 1.4.

BS 5750 systems

Basic concepts

All that I have written so far applies to any QA system.

Many organizations wish to have their QA systems approved by an external agency. The UK standard for QA systems is set by the British Standards Institution (BSI) and is called BS 5750. Since BS 5750 is a recognized international standard as well as a British one, it is often referred to by its international number, ISO 9000. This section introduces BS 5750/ISO 9000.

BS 5750 is a series of standards for QA systems. The separate parts of the series will be explained shortly. In the overall description of the series, BSI says, 'They identify the basic disciplines and specify the procedures and criteria to ensure that products or services meet the customers' requirements.' (BS 5750/ISO 9000:1987 A *Positive Contribution to Better Business*, p 4).

If you decide that you wish your QA system to have the BSI 'kite-mark', then you have to apply to have your system *registered*. This involves having your system *assessed* by an *approved assessor*.

You are probably familiar with other BSI standards, either because you use them, or because you have seen BS numbers on manufactured goods. For example, the plug on my desk lamp says, 'To BS 1363'. All these standards set specific quality criteria that the product must meet, eg covering the strengths of materials, size, fire resistance. BS 5750 is different from *all* these standards: nowhere does it specify a measurable quality standard. Instead, 'BS 5750 sets out how you can establish, document and maintain an effective quality system which will demonstrate to your customers that you are committed to quality and are able to supply their quality needs' (BS 5750/ISO 9000:1987 A *Positive Contribution to Better Business*, p 7). So, as I said at the start of this chapter, QA is really a management system. Given our long familiarity with British Standards, it can be hard to understand a standard that does not specify a quality level. How can such a standard control quality?

The answer is simple, if a little subtle. Buried in BS 5750

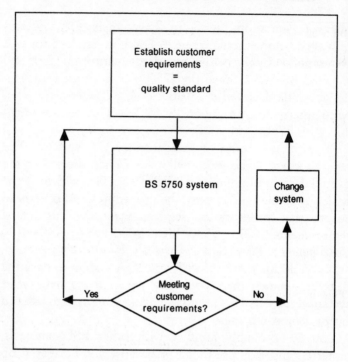

Figure 1.5 *How BS 5750 imposes a standard*

is the requirement that you accurately ascertain your customers' requirements. The QA system is, then, a management system for ensuring that your organization meets those requirements. So the quality standard is set after all, but by your customers, not by BSI. Figure 1.5 summarizes the concept in a very simple model of the BS 5750 system.

The series

BS 5750 is not a single standard, but a series of three standards:

- Part 1 (*Specification for design /development, production, installation and servicing for organizations*) for those

BS 5750	Education/training equivalent
Design/development	Curriculum development Course design Learning materials design
Production	Training/teaching Producing learning materials Tutoring Assessing Counselling
Installation	Setting up a course for a client to run at the client's site
Servicing	Follow-up of learners after course completion
Final inspection	Assessing/examining

Table 1.2 *Some BS 5750 terms and their training/ education equivalents*

organizations involved in design/development, production, installation and servicing.
- Part 2 (*Specification for production, and installation*) for those organizations making goods or providing services but *not* designing the goods or services.
- Part 3 (*Specification for final inspection and test*) for those organizations solely involved in final inspection and testing.

You have to decide which one of these parts best fits your organization. This is not immediately easy since the BS 5750 terminology is not easy to apply to training and education. Table 1.2 attempts to match training and education terminology against some of the key functions mentioned in BS 5750.

The following sets of questions are a guide to making the decision between Parts 1, 2 and 3.

31

A Does your organization design any part of the learning process as a *critical part* of its activity (eg curriculum development, design learning materials, design teaching materials)? If your answer is 'yes' then Part 1 applies to your organization.

B If your organization does not fit Part 1, does it teach or train learners as a critical part of its activity? If your answer is 'yes', then Part 2 applies to your organization.

C If neither Part 1 nor Part 2 applies to your organization then it neither designs any part of the teaching process nor delivers any part of it. Does your organization test learners? If your answer is 'yes', then Part 3 applies to it.

NB: if your organisation both tests learners and *designs* the tests which it uses, then Part 1 applies. Part 3 is a very restricted category which applies to perhaps less than 1 in 1000 training or educational establishments.

Part 1 applies to almost every training and education organization in the UK. The main exceptions are central teaching bodies with local teaching centres. If the local centres play no part in the design of the teaching, then those centres would be covered by Part 2; the main centre, designing the teaching programmes, would be covered by Part 1.

Parts 0, 4 and 8

Finally, the guideline parts: Parts 0, 4 and 8.

Part 0 is not a part of the standard in the sense that Parts 1, 2 and 3 are. Instead it is an overall guide to the concepts used in Parts 1, 2 and 3. This means that whichever of Parts 1, 2 or 3 you choose for your organization, you additionally need to read Part 0.

Part 4 is explained by its title, *Guide to the use of BS 5750*. It is again advisory, rather than part of the standard.

Similarly, Part 8, *Guide to quality management and quality systems elements for services*, is advisory only: it shows how you can use Parts 1, 2 and 3 in service industries rather than in manufacturing, for which they were originally designed. Part 8 is therefore particularly valuable in training and education, which are services rather than manufacture.

Part 1

From here on, this book will refer exclusively to Part 1 for two reasons:

- Part 1 is required by more than 99 per cent of training and teaching establishments.
- Parts 2 and 3 are simply Part 1 with various bits omitted, so the needs of Part 2 and 3 users will still be covered in this book.

What Part 1 covers

Because the language of BS 5750 is so alien to training and education, it is not helpful to simply list the Part 1 headings. I prefer to give my own overview of what you will find in Part 1, but translated into training and education terminology. The following is a sample of the sort of issues which BS 5750 will require you to consider.

- what management has to do in running a QA system;
- what a QA system is;
- how auditing should be done;
- checking your customers' requirements;
- controlling course/materials design;
- making sure you buy exactly what you need;
- keeping track of the learning process;
- using appropriate assessment methods;
- making sure inaccurate/out of date information and materials are not used;
- helping learners after course completion;

- keeping appropriate records;
- maintaining safe working practices.

Summary

In this chapter, I have looked at:

- why we need QA systems;
- the principles of QA systems;
- the basics of BS 5750.

It is now time to look at how you can begin to create a BS 5750 system for your organization.

Chapter 2

Setting up a Quality System

What a quality system is

Meeting the customers' requirements

It is all too common in education to find a course on offer simply because a lecturer wishes to teach it. In training, the same courses may be offered year after year just because the trainers feel comfortable delivering them. Less common was my experience of a university department that dropped electronics because the professor was tired of teaching it. These are all examples of product-driven organizations. 'We are good at Sanskrit, so we'll teach it.' Product-driven organizations can, and often do, offer very high quality services. The professional pride behind the product drive ensures commitment to doing a good job. Unfortunately, the result can be totally irrelevant to learners' needs. In the 'fitness for purpose' definition, product-driven is almost certainly low quality.

Introducing a QA system compels a move away from the product-driven approach. As Figure 1.5 highlighted, once you start down the BS 5750 route, the sole determinant of what should be provided and to what standard is the customer. A QA system is a management system for ensuring that an organization meets its customers' requirements. This immediately poses a problem in training and education: the 'customer' can be a complex amalgam of learner, employer, government agency and so on. However, these are all *external* to the organization and so together constitute the market and the customer. Somehow a way has to be found to balance all their demands into a single customer requirement.

BS 5750 requires that your organization:

- determines the need for its service;
- defines that need accurately and in enough detail to meet it;
- reviews the need during the process of meeting it ('contract review' in BS 5750 jargon);
- ensures that all the staff involved know what the need is.

Establishing customer needs

BS 5750 is not there to tell you *how* to determine what your market wants. You are totally free to choose any methods which can effectively deliver the requirements in the list above.

There are two aspects to determining the needs of your markets:

- the market research aspects;
- the QA aspects.

I will deal with these in turn.

The market research aspects

While BS 5750 requires you to determine the needs of your market, it is important to remember why you are doing this: you are doing it because you need the information in order to provide an effective service. *You are not*

36

doing it because BS 5750 tells you to do it. This latter point will be one which I will return to many times in this book. There is no point in meeting any of the requirements of BS 5750 if those requirements do not meet the needs of your organization and its customers. All the time, you have to keep asking, 'Is this right for us?'; 'Will this benefit our learners?' and so on.

So, in collecting market data, you will be doing so because you need the information. The information which you might decide you need could include:

Your existing customers

- How satisfied are they with your existing service?
- What are the strengths of your current service? (eg high pass rates, flexible service, good learning materials.)
- What are the weaknesses of your current service? (eg low pass rates, courses too inflexible.)
- From where else do your current customers buy training and education services?
- Are your existing customers thinking of buying more or less from you? More or less from your competitors?

Potential new customers

- Who are the potential customers? (eg companies, individuals, government schemes, voluntary bodies.)
- From where do these organizations currently get their training services?
- How satisfied are they with those services?
- If they were to switch suppliers, what would they be looking for in a new supplier? (eg cheaper service, higher qualification pass rates, more flexible service.)

In finding all this out, you have the usual wide range of market research and evaluation techniques available such as:

- postal and telephone surveys;
- interviews;
- researching published data;
- end of course surveys;
- course records.

None of this is specific to BS 5750 or to QA. Many organizations already carry out much of this type of data collation even if they have never thought of having a QA system. I will now turn to the QA-specific aspects of market information.

The QA aspects

The QA side of determining your customers' needs is all about being able to show that you have a system for determining needs, that the system is being followed and that the people who need the information are receiving it. If a training organization carried out a massive needs survey and then did no further research for five years, that would not meet BS 5750 requirements. Far better to have something small but regular which makes sure that you know about changing market trends. The emphasis is on being systematic.

A systematic approach to establishing market needs might start with a market research policy statement. This would state the basic approach that your organization takes to data collection. The statement could commit you to carrying out activities such as:

- an annual survey of a sample of corporate customers;
- a biennial survey of prospective new customers;
- end of course surveys of all learners.

It would also need to detail how the work was to be organized. For example, you might specify:

- a market-needs survey group to organize surveys;

- a format for collating data;
- a format for reports;
- circulation lists for different types of reports;
- management summaries to go to the QA management review group.

All of these ideas are my suggestions, not prescriptions laid down in BS 5750. They may not be right for your organization, in which case you just do what works for you. As long as you can demonstrate the following, you will meet BS 5750 requirements:

- your market is clearly defined;
- the needs of the market are regularly checked;
- those who design your courses and services receive the market data;
- there are systems for ensuring that the market data are used to define the services that you provide.

Management responsibilities

Quality policy

Management responsibility is central to BS 5750. If there is any suspicion that management – at all levels, including the highest – is not taking the QA system seriously, then your BS 5750 assessors will conclude that the system is not effective. This is summarized forcefully in Part 0:

The management of a company should develop and state its corporate quality policy. This policy should be consistent with other company policies. Management should take all necessary measures to ensure that its corporate quality policy is understood, implemented and maintained. (BS 5750: Part 0: Section 0.2: 1987)

There is a very practical reason for this insistence on management involvement. Since QA is itself a management system, and since an organization cannot run with two management systems, a QA system can only work with total senior management commitment.

I shall now look at the separate components of this BS 5750 statement.

Corporate quality policy

I touched on what this needs to cover in Chapter 1 and will now look at its practical implementation. As BS 5750 emphasizes, the quality policy has to be available to all staff and to be understood by them. This puts a premium on the quality policy being simple and clear. The detail is left to the system documentation as explained later in this chapter.

This short policy statement should be understandable by almost anyone who has an interest in your organization – learners, parents, lecturers, awarding bodies, employers. It needs to set out:

- the type of quality commitment which the organization makes to its learners, employers, etc;
- the broad methods which it takes to ensure that it meets that commitment;
- the systems available to put right omissions and errors (eg you may have appeals systems, exam or assessment re-marking systems);
- the broad responsibilities that different types of staff have for implementing the policy (eg 'All training staff are responsible for providing learners with regular feedback on their progress');
- how to find out more about the detail of the quality system.

Having created your quality policy, it also has uses outside BS 5750 requirements. For example, when bidding for contracts (eg with government training schemes) or in promoting your services (eg in your prospectus), it can be a very useful promotional device.

The quality system

It is one thing to have a policy, but quite another to turn it into a system that can deliver that policy. It is a management responsibility to devise, promulgate and monitor such a system. In one sense, everything that you do as part of your QA system is the quality system but here I am looking at the specification of that system and the documentation that goes with it.

Where does management start? First with the age-old question, 'What kind of a business are we really in?' and then with the new QA question, 'What is really critical?'

These two questions need to be asked and answered carefully in order to (a) avoid a blind and inappropriate application of BS 5750 (designed for manufacturing) to training and education, and (b) to prevent your system from tackling irrelevant detail. *For a QA system to work well, it is essential that it concentrates on the things which make a difference.* What might these be? Each organization is different, but these areas might prove critical in most training and education organizations:

- how market needs are identified;
- how needs are turned into curricular or course specifications;
- how learners are recruited and counselled;
- how learner progress is monitored;
- how learner achievement is assessed;
- how staff are selected;
- how staff are developed;
- how courses (rather than individual learners) are evaluated.

Once a list such as this has been compiled – almost certainly by a bottom-up process involving staff and learners at all levels – it is management's job to decide which items are critical and therefore the ones for which

41

there will be a QA policy. Most organizations make this initial list too long. Be warned!

You now have a list of critical functions. Next you need a policy. This will set out in broad terms the management's quality approach to each function. Eg, your policy for learner recruitment and counselling might be:

> All prospective learners shall receive written details of the courses in which they have expressed interest. These details shall include: the prior knowledge and skills assumed for the course, the course aims and objectives, the learning time, the methods of assessment, the qualification awarded and career/training routes available at the end of the course.
>
> Before enrolling, each learner shall be interviewed by an admissions' counsellor.

This is a policy statement and is therefore short on operational detail. For each of these functions that you have decided are critical, your policy statement will be followed by the writing of a detailed operational procedure (see below). Although it is right to keep your quality policy under regular review, you don't want to find it full of transient detail which requires frequent updating. You need to aim for a balance between being too vague for the policy to mean anything and too detailed for it to be policy.

Quality review

The final management role is the quality review. I have emphasized the self-adjusting nature of QA systems. The management review is the engine for that process. At its simplest, the review needs to decide:

- What do we need to know to be sufficiently certain that our QA policy is being implemented?
- What do we need to know to decide whether the policy needs amendment?

• How frequently does this data need to be collected?

As ever, it is important to decide what is critical and genuinely indicative of the health of the QA system. The more data management asks for, the less it will be able to make sense of it. Equally account must be taken of the cost of data collection. The more that management asks for data that is not automatically collected as part of day-to-day work, the more the costs of the QA system will rise. The efficient and economic way to resolve this is to scan the procedures once they have been written in order to identify data that will be in the system which is of value in assessing the overall health of the QA system. There will, however, be data of two types:

• operational data (eg course completion rates, award rates, absentee rates, repeat business rates);
• QA system data (eg percentage of audits completed on time).

The management review should contain a sensible balance between the two. There should be enough to convince management that nothing *critical* could be going wrong, but no more.

The quality system loop

A final way to check on the management role is to look at the quality loop and ask whether you have thought of everything on it. Once again, the basic loop in BS 5750 is very hard to interpret for training and education, so, in Figure 2.1, I have presented my interpretation of the loop.

System components

Procedures

In the quality policy, you have identified all the main

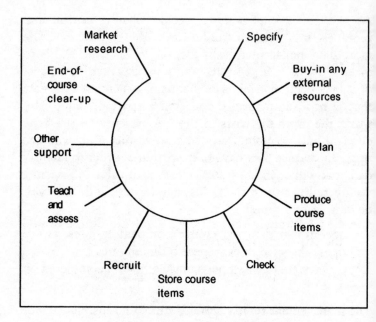

Figure 2.1 *The quality loop*
(adapted from BS 5750 Part 0)

functions that you wish to control as part of the QA system. Because the policy statements are far too broad to be used for day-to-day implementation by staff, a procedure is written for each function. In operational terms, the procedures are the most important documents since they are the ones which control most day-to-day actions and – very important – set down who does what.

In this section, I outline the main purposes of procedures, how they are composed and how they are used.

A procedure sets out for one function:

- the main steps in that function with special emphasis on the critical interfaces;
- who is responsible for carrying out each function;

44

- the quality standard to which each stage should be taken;
- the form in which work is to be handed from one stage to another;
- the quality records which have to be retained to show that the work was done to the procedure.

Once the procedure is written and agreed, staff follow it as the agreed way of working.

However well staff know and understand the QA policy, their immediate reference will be one or more procedures. It is therefore critical that procedures satisfy a number of criteria:

- they accurately reflect how the job should be done if the customers' requirements are to be met;
- they are easily understood;
- tasks are described clearly in terms of what will be the outcome;
- responsibilities are clearly defined.

For example, the following is poorly worded:

Learners shall be regularly tested.

If you had to check up whether this wording had been followed, you would not know:

- how often 'regularly' is;
- what evidence to accept to show that testing has been done;
- who should have done the testing.

Here is the same sentence reworded with the kind of precision required in a procedure:

At least once a month, trainers shall test each of their learners using one of the tests from the approved test bank. The results shall be recorded by the trainer in the learner's log.

From this it is clear:

- *when* the task is to be done – at least once a month;
- *who* carries out the task – the learner's trainer;
- *what* the outcome is – a result recorded in the learner's log.

For every QA task, it should be easy to identify:

- what the outcome is;
- who does it;
- when they do it.

Anything that fails these three tests has to be rethought.

Work instructions

One thing that procedures should never do is to describe *how* a task should be done. If that level of detail were allowed into procedures, they would become so dense as to be useless. It is at this point that work instructions take over.

Work instructions can be *very* detailed – if that is necessary. Their function is to specify precise detail where precise detail is needed. Table 2.1 suggests some possible procedure items where a corresponding detailed work instruction might be needed.

Creating a good work instruction is often a matter of considering who will use it and *how* it will be used. For example, consider the task of producing a course specification. You could write a lengthy prose guide to tell someone how to do the job. Would they read it? Probably not. Would they follow it when doing the job? Even less likely. The solution is to turn your instructions into a job-aid. This makes the user keen to follow the work instruction since to do so makes the job easier. For these reasons, almost all work instructions are in one of the following forms:

46

Procedure item	Possible work instruction
Provide job placement	Checklist for placement interview
Produce course specification	Checklist of items to include
Pre-course advice	Checklist of questions to ask
Record assessment result	Pro-forma for recording the assessment

Table 2.1 *Work instructions amplifying procedure tasks*

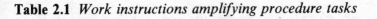

- a form to fill in (eg an exam entry form);
- a checklist of points (eg a list of points to check in preparing a training room for a training session);
- a list of headings (eg the headings under which to collect data for a course specification);
- a diagram to show how to do a task (eg how to lay out a page of text for a presentation).

Not only are such work instruction formats very easy to follow but they are themselves a natural part of the work. Wherever QA can use natural working documents and data, the better.

Auditing

The whole management review system and the self-improving nature of QA systems demand that the system is continually under check to see whether it is performing to plan. This checking process is called *auditing* since the methods which it uses are very similar to those of financial auditing.

Auditing works by regularly checking through each

Month	Procedures to audit
January	Admissions
February	Course specifications
March	Training delivery
April	Assessment systems

Table 2.2 *An extract from an audit timetable*

procedure to see whether the work is being done as set out in the procedure. Any deviations are recorded as *non-compliances* which then have to be put right. The process of putting right a non-compliance is called *corrective action.*

The auditing process requires auditors. Except in the largest organizations, auditing is just an additional task that the organizations' staff take on. Trainers, managers, secretaries, administrators and technical staff can all take on the role of auditing for, say, a week or so a year. These people will all require training in auditing (see Chapter 6).

Through the quality management system, a timetable is drawn up which ensures that all the procedures are audited on a regular basis. For example, the most important procedures might be audited twice a year while the less important ones are done once a year. Table 2.2 shows an extract from a typical audit timetable.

For each procedure, one or more auditors is appointed. When the time comes to audit that procedure, the auditor visits the section using the procedure and, in an auditing meeting, works step by step through each statement in the procedure checking the evidence that the step has been applied.

It is at this point that the difference between a good or bad procedure can often become apparent. In a bad procedure, precisely what evidence constitutes compliance may be very unclear. In a good procedure, the nature of evidence of compliance should be obvious. For example,

The trainer shall agree a list of performance outcomes with the client company

is vague since it does not say what constitutes evidence of 'agreed'. If the procedure is reworded, this vagueness can be removed:

The trainer shall prepare a list of performance outcomes agreed with and signed by the client company.

It is now clear that the auditor will be looking for the signed list. These clear-cut pieces of evidence are called *quality records* and they are discussed in more detail in the next section.

Quality records

It is clear that successful auditing depends on evidence being available to show that the procedure has – or has not – been followed. Anything which is used to record compliance is called a *quality record*.

It is possible to introduce a QA system which specifies all sorts of new and complex records which will have to be kept as quality records. This is not the way to introduce QA. It results in deep resentment from all the staff who have to run the QA system while fortifying the belief that QA is just a load of paper.

An efficient and successful QA system will seek every opportunity to use everyday working documents as quality records. Almost certainly, the existing document formats will need some tightening in order to become quality records, but the important thing is that the number of documents does not increase. Table 2.3 gives some exam-

Everyday document	Process for which it can be a quality record
Signed course specification	Completion of specification process
Learner's computer record	Pre-course data collection
Learner portfolio signed record	Completion of competence assessment

Table 2.3 *Examples of quality records*

ples of how everyday documents might become quality records for various processes.

Corrective action

While everyone might hope that the auditing will reveal complete compliance, non-compliances are not unusual – especially in a new system. The corrective action process is the means through which the non-compliance is put right. BS 5750 requires a QA system to have a systematic method for corrective action. This will be something like:

At the time of the audit

- auditor and auditee agree in writing the factual nature of the non-compliance (eg learner's portfolio had not been signed by assessor);
- the auditee writes down what action will be taken to correct the non-compliance (eg assessor to be asked to sign the portfolio);
- the auditee agrees by when this will be done (eg within two weeks).

After the audit meeting

- the auditee corrects the non-compliance;
- the auditor follows-up the agreed action at the end of the agreed period to see if the action is complete.

There is no guarantee that the corrective action will have been taken at the end of the agreed period, so the QA system has to have a means of acting on failure to implement corrective action. This would normally involve the auditor reporting the omission to someone higher up the management chain. The full audit cycle is described in Figure 2.2.

Management review

Day in, day out, staff will be carrying out tasks and functions according to the agreed QA procedures and work instructions. At regular intervals – perhaps once a month – some part or other of the procedures will be under audit. The whole process becomes an integral part of how work is done and how it is managed. However, just as any course or training system needs to be evaluated from time to time, so does any QA system. This evaluation process is called management review.

Management review should be second nature to trainers and educators since it follows the basic principles of evaluating any on-going training and education system. In training/education language, we would say:

- Are we meeting our objectives?
- If not, what action do we need to take?
- Do our objectives need to be changed?

The QA management review follows a similar format:

- Are we implementing the procedures?
- If not, what action do we need to take?
- Do our procedures need to be changed?

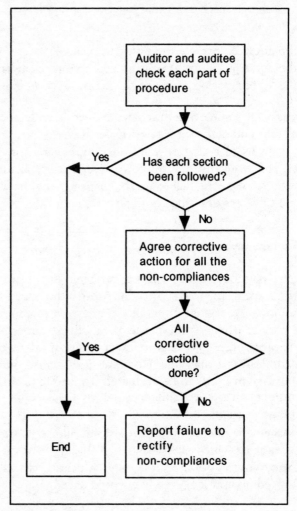

Figure 2.2 *The auditing process*

As with any evaluation system, if you do not take early steps to collect the data as you go along, it may be difficult, expensive or even impossible to collect the data later. That is particularly serious in QA since, if you cannot prove that you are complying with the procedures, the assumption has to be that you are not. No news is bad news in QA. This

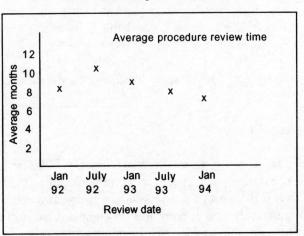

Figure 2.3 *A management review chart*

means that management must be explicit about the data which it wishes to evaluate in its reviews. This will tend to be of two types: routine statistical data and *ad hoc* surveys. The sorts of data that management might seek include:

- percentage of audits carried out within one week of target date;
- number of non-compliances detected per audit;
- percentages of corrective actions carried out within the time period agreed between auditor and auditee;
- what percentage of total non-compliances belong to each procedure;
- average length of time since each procedure was last reviewed;
- number of procedures not reviewed in the last twelve months.

All these types of data are easily plotted on time graphs so that management can see the trend in performance. Figure 2.3 shows a typical graph of this type.

The other category of data which a management review group might seek is *ad hoc* reports. For example, the group might wish to review:

53

- trainers' views on how well the QA system supports them in their day to day work;
- suppliers' views of the QA system;
- a sample of QA systems in similar establishments.

Contract review

The term *contract review* comes from BS 5750 and is a typical example of a piece of manufacturing terminology which it is difficult to translate into training and education. In manufacturing, it is common for the manufacturer to be making something which has been very precisely commissioned by a customer – often another manufacturer or an assembly company. Hence most of the work of manufacturers is dominated by the contracts which specify what is to be produced and to what quality. In training and education, the situation is often less clearly defined.

As with any part of BS 5750, you are only required to implement it in so far as it is relevant to the nature of your organization and the needs of your customers. I shall therefore discuss contract review in the sort of training and education situation where it is clearly relevant.

Consider the case where a training supplier has received a contract to supply a programme of training for a group of supervisors. BS 5750 then obliges the supplier to carry out three tasks:

- to make sure that the customer's requirement is 'adequately defined and documented';
- if the customer has changed his or her requirement since any earlier specification, that this has been taken account of;
- to check that the organization has the resources to fulfil the contract.

So, in the context of the hypothetical supervisory management case, you would need to check:

- that you have enough details of:
  - the learners and their current skills and knowledge;
  - the learning outcomes they are to achieve;
  - when and where they will be available for teaching and learning;
  - the resources to be supplied by the client, etc.
- that your latest understanding of the requirement is written down and signed by the client;
- that you have the right resources such as:
  - staff with the right skills
  - you are registered with the appropriate awarding body;
  - you have the right training rooms;
  - you have appropriate learning materials, and so on.

It all sounds obvious – QA usually is – but so often we can all think of examples of when such basic planning steps were not taken.

Obtaining BS 5750

You can choose whether to seek external recognition of your QA system. If you decide that you want external recognition, then you must have your system assessed against the BS 5750 standards.

As you have seen, BSI issue the 5750 standard in the UK. Separately, a number of bodies are approved to assess organizations against BS 5750. These are called certification bodies. Currently there are about 15 in the UK. The role of a certification body is to assess in depth your quality system in order to see whether it meets the standards set out in BS 5750. You pay the certification body a fee, negotiated in the light of the size of your organization and the complexity of your QA system. For certification, you will be asked to submit your Quality Manual and procedures but, apart from that, documentation is kept very simple. The certifying body then:

- reviews your QA documentation;
- visits your premises to interview QA staff, interview other staff and generally see the QA system in practice;
- produces a report which either confirms that you have met the standard or advises you of the changes needed in your system to meet the standard.

Putting the certification process alongside the other steps in this chapter, the full steps in obtaining BS 5750 are as follows:

1 Obtain the parts of BS 5750 which you need from BSI.
2 Design your system as set out in this book. (In practice, you will probably need the help of an external consultant for this step.)
3 Choose a certification body.
4 Certification body visit.
5 Receive certification or amend your system.

Choosing a certification body

You can obtain a list of certification bodies from BSI or from the National Accreditation Council for Certification Bodies (NACCB). Their addresses are in the Bibliography and Addresses section at the end of this book. In choosing a certification body, it is best to look for one with plenty of experience of your type of organization. The more they understand your type of business, the better they will understand the subtleties of adapting BS 5750 to your work. It is also a good idea to check with organizations similar to your own which have achieved BS 5750 which certifying body they used and what their experience was. If you do choose a certifying body with a poor track record in your type of business, you can expect a difficult time as they adapt to your specific needs.

Summary

That completes a very quick run through the working tools of a QA system. It is now time to look at exactly which parts of your work have to be covered by procedures if you are to meet BS 5750.

In Chapter 3 I shall systematically work through the sections of BS 5750 Part 1, showing to what they equate in training and education.

Once that task is complete, the remaining chapters will go on to cover the detailed skills needed to set up a QA system.

Chapter 3

The Requirements of BS 5750

Introduction

In this chapter I shall work through the remaining sections of BS 5750 Part 1, ie sections 4.4 to 4.20. (Sections 4.1 to 4.3 have been covered in Chapter 2.) The main purpose in doing this is to try to make Part 1 relevant to training and education. With a plethora of phrases such as 'design control', 'verification of purchased product' and 'inspection and test status', it is easy to assume that all this has nothing to do with training and education. Superficially, it hasn't; considerable delving is needed to identify the training and education equivalents of the requirements set out in section 4 of Part 1. There is also the extensive additional guidance in Part 8 of the standard; this interprets the standard for service industries.

It is, however, important to keep the aims and needs of your organization in perspective when applying BS 5750. You are not required to blindly follow all its requirements if those requirements are irrelevant to the needs of your customers or conflict with your customers' needs. This is one reason why it is so important to assess the needs of your customers. When a BS 5750 assessor is assessing your system, he/she may challenge you on the way in which you do something. If you can produce clear evidence that your practice is in the interests of your customers, then the assessor's challenge must fail. This will, I hope, become clearer as I work through section 4.

One final point about section 4: once you have decided which items do apply to your organization, you will have to decide how to incorporate them within your procedures. Some parts of section 4 (eg Design and Development Planning) are so important that you may decide to have a whole procedure devoted to them. Other parts are less important in training and education (eg Servicing) so you may decide to incorporate them within some other procedure. As you go through this chapter, you may find it helpful to note the relative importance of each section as a preliminary to deciding which BS 5750 sections merit whole procedures.

The heading in this chapter for each BSI section shows the relevant BSI Part 0 section number, eg 4.4.

This chapter is considerably longer than the other chapters in this book. I could have split it up, but any break-point would have been entirely artificial. BS 5750 Part 1 is a single set of 20 standards, each being in some way connected to the others. I have therefore kept all the sections together in the one chapter.

In reading this chapter, you may wish to have a copy of the Part 1 standard to hand. However, the chapter is self-contained and a copy of the standard is not essential.

Design control (4.4)

What is design control?

BS 5750 requires organizations to have 'procedures to control and verify the design of the product in order to ensure that the specified requirements are met'. In manufacture, 'design' is every stage from an initial idea for a new product through to the detailed plans from which that product will be machined. This section of BS 5750, however, uses the words *design control* and not just design. This emphasizes the need for the whole process of design to be under control. It is not enough to, somehow or other, produce the right product in the end: it must be produced through an orderly and organized approach.

Design control in training and education

To identify what design control in education and training is, we first need to identify what the product is that education and training produces. This requires an important digression.

The training and education product

If you decide to take a course (or are sent on one), you are purchasing a product/service from a training or education organization. What do you expect to get for your money? Your list is likely to be something like:

- master something by the end of the course as evidenced by a certificate and your capacity to do something;
- receive help during the course with any learning problems which you have;
- access to resources to help you learn – rooms, equipment, audio-visual aids, books, etc;
- receive teaching input – which may come from a tutor or from learning resources.

What is clear from this list is that the product of training and education is in two distinct parts:

- process (the *experience* of learning);
- product (what you have *achieved* at the end).

If, as trainers and educators, we wish to be in full control of our product, then we need to be in control of the quality of the process that we offer learners and the quality of their

60

final achievement. We cannot control either of these if we do not have a design process to plan what will be offered.

The design process revisited

It should now be clear that in training and education, the design process is *course planning*, including planning the teaching of the courses.

Why design control is needed

All trainers and teachers would avow their personal commitment to promising a quality service. Quality assurance goes beyond that avowal to seek methods by which the quality can be systematically guaranteed rather than arise solely from personal commitment. Nowhere is that assurance more important than in the design stage. If an organization plans the wrong courses, whatever the quality of the delivery, they will still be the wrong courses. Given the tendency of trainers and educators to take a teacher-driven view of their work, there is a double importance to having an effective design system.

The main purpose of the design system is to take the identified needs of the customer and to develop a way of meeting these. Anything which will be used to meet the customer's needs and has to be designed is covered by this section. That could include:

- curriculum plans
- course plans
- handouts
- learning materials
- assessment materials
- work placements
- course visits

There is no definitive list. You have to decide for each of your courses what are those aspects which need design.

The principles of design control

BS 5750 identifies five aspects to design control. These are:

- design and development planning – deciding who does what in the design system;
- design input – making sure the designers know what the customer wants;
- design output – being clear about the final form your plans should take;
- design verification – checking with your customer that the design solution is acceptable;
- design changes – having a system to ensure that any changes to the design are approved by the right people.

Applying design control

To apply BS 5750 design requirements to training and education, we have to take each of the five aspects and identify their appropriate application.

Design and development planning

In any organization and for any function, who does what has to be clear. Here you are required to draw up plans for products (courses, etc) and to identify responsibilities for those plans. Teaching organizations often do this at many levels (eg at department level and at course level) but I will illustrate the concept at course level. First, you need a list of all the critical tasks that go into developing a course plan; then you need to identify what the output of that task is; and then you have to decide who is responsible for carrying it out. Table 3.1 illustrates how the planning system might work in a training organization.

Any scheme for your organization may be very different from this. What matters is that, in your scheme, you have specified:

- all the critical tasks;
- what the output of each task is;

Task	Output	Who
Agree requirement with customer	Customer specification	Head of Training
Write training session plans	Training session plans	Course tutor
Write assessment items	Assessment items	Course tutor
Write handouts	Handout manuscript	Course tutor
Design handouts	Handout masters	DTP section
Print handouts	Handouts	Print section

Table 3.1 *Design tasks for a training course*

- who is to carry out the task.

A digression on output

Since this is the first application of section 4 to training and education, another new concept has arisen: the importance of outputs. QA is about *assurance*, which means being able to check up that something has been done. We cannot check on a process (like 'writing course specification') but we can check up on the end result of a process (like 'finished course specification'). Time and again you will find that the output of a process is emphasised in QA. That should be all very familiar to trainers and educators where we so frequently emphasize learning outputs rather than the learning process.

Design input

You are required to identify the 'design input requirements' and to check that you have enough information to design the product. You can do this course by course, but it is far more efficient to design a standard checklist which all your staff can use and then to incorporate this checklist as a work instruction for your procedure on design control. The checklist will specify the sort of things which you would normally expect to know before designing a course, eg:

- characteristics of the learners (age, sex, educational level, jobs, etc);
- the learning outcomes to be achieved;
- external award to be aimed at;
- when and where learning is to take place;
- number of hours available for study;
- types of learning with which learners are familiar (face-to-face, distance learning, etc);
- types of support available to learner (eg line manager, mentor).

This list is not meant to be definitive – a list I frequently use runs to four sides of A4 – but to indicate the nature of a systematic checklist for design input.

Design output

The BS 5750 requirements for design output are highly technical, but essentially boil down to saying that the output must:

- match the input requirement;
- make the criteria used explicit;
- meet any legal requirements.

In this form, the list is fairly explicit but *however obvious the list may appear, you still have to build the stage into your procedure.* In other words, your design procedure is expected to have a stage at which the design is checked for these requirements.

Design verification

Having carried out your design, you have to have a system for verifying that it is acceptable. Be warned: this is a typical area where slavish adherence to BS 5750 can lead to you introducing new and cumbersome systems which are not necessary. Design verification for a typical training course may simply mean sending the customer two copies and asking him/her to return one signed copy to indicate acceptance of the course design. If this is really not enough for your type of work, by all means read the small print of 4.4.5, but do not implement it unless your customers' requirements cannot be implemented without it.

Design changes

Even the most carefully designed course may have to be changed after the initial design is approved. Customers change their requirements, learner groups can turn out to be different from the ones originally destined to take the course, and so on. BS 5750 allows for all this by requiring you to have a system for identifying when changes are needed and for making and recording those changes. For most types of training provision, all that is required is a means of:

- reviewing the course occasionally to see if the need has changed (eg a mid-point review);
- specifying where the changes are to be recorded;
- specifying who is to receive a copy of the changes.

Document control (4.5)

What is document control?

Basically, document control is making sure that everyone has up-to-date copies of those documents that they need.

However, BS 5750 document control is only concerned with those documents which are required by BS 5750 itself. After reading the next few pages, you may decide that you could usefully apply document control beyond the mandatory requirements of BS 5750.

A simple example of document control occurs every day at your newsagent's. You expect your newsagent to keep a list of who is to receive which newspaper, to make sure that today's papers are sent out (and not yesterday's), and to check that the rounds have been done. A newsagent without document control would not stay in business for long.

In a more complex way, BS 5750 requires you to:

- identify which documents need to be controlled documents;
- only to issue controlled documents which have been checked by approved personnel;
- make sure the controlled documents are available to those who need them;
- have an effective method of removing obsolete controlled documents from circulation;
- keep master lists of who is to receive which controlled document.

Document control in training and education

There is nothing different about document control in training and education compared to other industries but there are areas of training and education where the principles of document control are already applied. For instance, the circulation of public examination papers and the later handling of completed scripts is all carefully recorded.

However experienced your organization is in document control, you are still likely to hear the repeated criticism that QA systems generate too much unnecessary paperwork. If you remember that the test of any QA action is, 'Is this necessary in order to meet my customers' requirements?', it will help in identifying just which paperwork is essential. The commonest categories of QA documentation are:

- procedures;
- work instructions;
- specifications;
- quality records.

Procedures, work instructions and specifications are likely to be controlled documents.

The principles of document control

Document control is the careful application of a set of principles which ensure that:

The document issuer

- has authorized the latest issue;
- knows who has copies of the document;
- knows obsolete copies have been destroyed.

The document users

- know which is the latest edition of the document;
- can see the edition number on their copy;
- can see the authorization signature on their copy.

All this is best explained by considering an example. An organization decides to introduce a new spreadsheet training course. Several tutors will teach the course at different times and several sales personnel will be selling the course. All these people need to have copies of the course specification. The specification itself will change from time to time.

Control process	Application
Identify document editions	Each edition of the specification has a version number and date on it
Issue authorized editions only	Each edition signed by course tutor before issue
Identify users	Keep list of tutors and sales staff
Circulate to users	Send each new revision to list of tutors and sales staff
Remove obsolete editions	Ask users to confirm destruction of out of date specification

Table 3.2 *Controlled issue of a course specification*

Table 3.2 illustrates how document control is applied to the course specification.

Purchasing (4.6)

What is purchasing?

In the BS 5750 context, purchasing is obtaining any goods or services *which are critical to your service as perceived by your customers* from any external supplier.

Purchasing in training and education

The purchasing process can be very important or fairly trivial in training and education according to whether you classify your part-time tutors as 'suppliers' or as 'staff'. If you decide to classify them as suppliers, then the purchasing section applies to them. If you classify them as 'staff', then 4.18 (training) applies to them. I shall assume that you classify your part-time tutors as staff and therefore exclude them from this section.

That leaves only a fairly small range of items that you are likely to purchase externally, including:

- learning materials;
- consultancy;
- external examiners and assessors;
- awarding body services.

To each of these, you are required to apply the principles of QA purchasing.

The principles of purchasing

These are simply stated.

Suppliers

- shall only be selected if they can demonstrate that they can meet your requirements;
- shall keep whatever records you require to show that they are meeting your requirements.

Purchasing documents

- are fully explicit as to what it is you wish to purchase and to what standard.

Because of the requirement to carefully control the service which your suppliers give you, normal QA practice is to keep a list of *approved suppliers*. Approved suppliers are ones who:

- have been checked by you and found able to meet your requirements;
- know your quality standards;

69

• agree to prove to you that they are following your systems.

Applying purchasing

I will assume that an organization has found that it needs suppliers under the four headings: learning materials, consultancy, assessors, and awarding bodies. For each of these categories, the organization then needs to identify and/or specify:

• the standard of performance required;
• the selection process;
• the records it wishes the suppliers to keep;
• the resulting list of approved suppliers.

As an example, consider the need to purchase external assessment services. Their assessments will only be accepted in the world at large if the assessors are fully qualified for the work they are to carry out. A careful selection (purchasing) system is needed to ensure this. Such a system is illustrated in Table 3.3.

Purchaser supplied product (4.7)

What is purchaser supplied product?

Wedding dresses are often made by freelance dressmakers. Quite often, the bride will choose and buy the fabric, taking it along to the dressmaker to make the dress. In this context, the fabric is *purchaser supplied product* – something the purchaser buys, supplies and owns, but which eventually becomes part of the product which the purchaser buys from the supplier.

Purchaser supply in training and education

Training and education organizations rarely, if ever, encounter purchaser supplied product, so most can argue

Requirement	Application
Decide standards	Assessors must: • have a professional qualification in the skill being assessed • hold an assessor's qualification from a national awarding body
Selection system	Applicants to: • complete application form • produce copies of certificates • produce two references • be interviewed by a course tutor
Records	Assessors to keep for two years: • records on centre forms of all assessments • any work items supplied by learners

Table 3.3 *Example of approved supplier system*

that they have no need for a procedure to cover this area. The few rare instances when it applies include:

- a customer who supplies training manuals to be used on a course;
- a customer who supplies equipment to be used on a course.

The principles of purchaser supply control

In essence, the BS 5750 requirement for purchaser supplied product is 'look after it – it's not yours'. More specifically, it requires you to:

- check you have been sent the right product;
- store it carefully;
- report back to your customer any loss or damage.

71

Requirement	Manuals case	Equipment case
Ensure correct items supplied	Check manuals for content and issue date	Check correct machine type Check machines work correctly Check all accessories supplied
Store safely	Provide suitable storage facilities with appropriate security Label as customer's property	Locate in safe location Ensure no unauthorized access Disable when not in use Have serviced if needed
Report loss/damage	Have system to check the materials regularly Have system to report any damage	Have system to check machine routinely Have system to report any damage

Table 3.4 *Applications of purchaser supplied product control*

Applying purchaser supply control

The two most likely areas where this might apply are the supply of manuals and the supply of equipment. Table 3.4 suggests how you might comply with BS 5750 in each of these cases.

Product identification and traceability (4.8)

What is product identification and traceability?

You will have seen mark numbers on many products. The one with which we are all increasingly familiar is the version number on software. My DTP programme is 'version 4.2'. This clearly identifies all the characteristics of my copy of the DTP programme. All other copies of version 4.2 of the programme are identical to mine; all copies of the programme that are not the same as mine will have different version numbers. Back at the manufacturer's, there will be a complete written specification of version 4.2 of the programme which exactly describes my package. This is *product identification*.

Similarly, you will have seen batch numbers on some goods – especially medicines. Perhaps 500 doses of a vaccine bear the batch number 839832. All those doses with the number 839832 will have been made in the vat (or however it is made) at the same time. If one dose of 839832 is found to be faulty, all the doses with that number are assumed to be faulty and are withdrawn. Through the batch number, the exact manufacture history of the dose is known and traceable. This is *product traceability*.

Product identification and traceability in training and education

Product identification

Here, training and education have two principle products to which identification applies:

- the course taken by the learner;
- the award given to the learner.

It is fairly obvious that teaching organizations need to keep records of which courses have been taught, eg at one centre, last year's courses included Management Information Systems Level 1 and Resource Management Level 2. Product identification means linking these titles with the written specifications of what each of those courses comprises.

Less obviously, both courses and awards vary from time

to time. This year's course on a company's appraisal system may be different from last year's course – perhaps the appraisal system has itself changed. *If* your courses vary enough from offer to offer, then course identification may need to extend to include the version, eg Resource Management Level 2 (version 3).

Traceability

It is not enough to know exactly what courses are on offer and what they contain: we need to know which learners took which course. A customer might come back and complain about 'your word processing course'. But which one? You offer six different types of word processing course, twice a year in each case. There needs to be a mechanism which ties each learner to each course – providing traceability. Fortunately there is and it is called learner records.

Applying product identification and traceability

This is one area of BS 5750 where existing learner records are likely to meet all requirements. If you can tick everything on the following list, you need take no further QA action.

Course numbering

- courses have unique titles or course numbers;
- each course offering can be separately identified.

Learner records

- show the courses taken by each learner including the particular offering.

74

Process control (4.9)

What is process control?

This is one of the areas where manufacture and training are superficially so very different. The quality of the car you buy depends on the design, the quality of the materials used and *how it is put together* – process control. This section of BS 5750 refers to *everything* in the manufacture and assembly of the product which *directly affects quality*. So, in manufacture this includes:

- the working methods used;
- the equipment used (tools, etc);
- how the work is monitored;
- the skills of the workforce.

Process control in training and education

To apply this section to training and education, we first have to identify what constitutes 'process'. The heart of process is everything that we normally refer to as teaching, training, tutoring and assessment. This comprises a wide range of activities including:

- teaching (the presentation of material);
- tutoring (assisting individual learners with learning difficulties);
- feedback to the learner;
- monitoring learner progress;
- adjusting the course to individual learner progress and needs (or moving the learner on to some other course);
- assessment of the learner;
- maintaining suitable records of learner progress.

In other words, absolutely anything which we expect teachers to do during the teaching process (as opposed to

75

the preparation process or the evaluation stage) and which is critical to quality, is covered by process control.

Applying process control

To apply process control to training and education, you have to ask, 'What are the processes for which we need to lay down standards, prescribe methods or monitor activity?' But . . . to start in that way is to overlook the most important aspect of process control in training and education: the quality of the staff.

Staff and process control

BS 5750 refers to staff skills ('workmanship') as part of process control and the wording leaves the impression that it is a minor contributor to ensuring a quality product. In a service activity such as training and education, the skills and quality of the teaching staff are the foremost determiners of a quality process. This is fully recognized in Part 8 of BS 5750 where, in discussing the differences between manufacture and service, it states, 'A most important resource in any organization is that of the individual members of personnel involved'.

This means that any process control procedure should put special emphasis on ensuring that the right staff are selected in the first place and that their continuing development needs are monitored and met. It also means that you have to be especially careful not to write a process control procedure which attempts to substitute endless checks and routines for simply having good staff in the first place.

In this context, a process control list for training and education would have to cover:

- standards for staff selection (eg the qualifications they are required to have);

- how the continuing relevance of staff skills is monitored;
- how staff development needs are met.

Additionally, you would have to decide which of the following need process control:

- teaching methods;
- tutoring methods;
- how feedback is given to learners;
- how learner progress is monitored;
- how checks are made to ensure learner needs are still being met by the course they are on;
- how learners are assessed;
- which learner records are kept.

In each case, what you are deciding – in addition to whether to control that function at all – is:

- do we need a work instruction for this function? (eg a specified learner record format);
- do we need to specify when/how often a function shall be carried out? (eg learners shall be assessed at least once a month);
- do we need to specify the standard to which something should be done?

Potentially process control is the most contentious area for training and education. Traditionally we have simply appointed suitably qualified staff and left them to get on with the job. There is a temptation to continue in that vein. To do that is too complacent, but equally to overprescribe how teaching shall be carried out is pointless – too much in teaching is about responding to unpredictable needs of learners. Again, BS 5750 Part 8 recognizes that much of a service process cannot be specified in prescriptive detail but that quality can be assured through staff selection and development.

One way of resolving *how much* to prescribe is to think of

the teaching process from the customer's point of view. Write down a list of what you promise to give the customer in terms of teaching process and then consider, 'How can we make sure we deliver what we have promised?' That 'making sure' is process control.

Inspection and testing (4.10)

What is inspection and testing?

Some interpreters of BS 5750 for training and education have described the learner as the product. To me this is repulsive. A product is 'a thing produced through a natural process of manufacture' (OED) so in no sense can the term be applied to a learner. But, for those who insist on labelling learners as the product, this section would then refer to assessing learners. Since I do not intend to call learners products, I shall restrict this section to the inspection of items used in the teaching process.

Inspection and testing is in three main parts in BS 5750: receiving, in-process and final inspection. I shall use these same divisions.

Receiving

This section requires you to check all incoming product before it is used – with the usual caveat that you will only need to check items that are critical to the quality as perceived by the customer.

In-process

This section requires you to check the product while it is under development, following whatever quality checks you have specified in your procedures. It also introduces a key

78

term in QA – non-conforming product. Non-conforming product is anything partly or fully made which has failed to meet the standards which you have set. It is a term which easily fits physical items (a handout which has been badly photocopied might be a non-conforming item) but is less easily applied to services such as teaching. The key point in BS 5750 about non-conforming product is that you must have a system for identifying and setting aside such product so as to prevent its accidental use.

Final inspection and test

Again, a concept which is much easier to apply to a physical product than to a service. This section requires you to check products for conformance to specification before they are released for use. Teaching, being a continuous process of manufacture and delivery in one go, cannot be inspected before release to the customer.

Inspection and testing in training and education

The service as perceived by the learner is broadly made up of physical items such as learning materials and the non-tangible teaching and assessment processes. Checking the quality of the teaching and assessment processes is already covered under process control above so the only aspects of inspection and testing left to cover here are physical components of the product or the physical items used to make a product (eg the paper used in making teaching materials).

There are a number of possible items which you might wish to consider for inspection and testing:

- bought-in learning materials (eg textbooks, audio/visual items);
- bought-in assessment materials;

Type of item	Test for	When
Learning materials	Correct item Complete Damage free	On delivery
Assessment materials	Correct item Complete Damage free	On delivery
Raw materials for student projects, etc	Meet specification	On delivery
Raw materials for organization's own manufacture eg paper	Meet specification	On delivery

Table 3.5 *Examples of receiving and testing incoming materials*

- bought-in materials on which learners work (eg electronic components, biological specimens);
- bought-in materials used to manufacture items in the organization (eg paper, ink).

Overall this is an area of BS 5750 where great caution should be exercised. In training and education, bought-in items play a small part in the overall service provided. Consequently, inspection and testing in this area can be an expensive use of time with little final benefit. As with all QA activities, you have to ask, 'Will this make enough difference to the customer to be worth doing?'

Applying inspection and testing

Once you have decided your list of items to inspect and test, you then have to specify a system. Table 3.5 gives some examples of such a system.

It is a relevant point to note that BS 5750 is not concerned with money. The QA systems which BS 5750 mandates you to install are not required to check whether you have paid for your purchases, or even paid too much for them. You check for quality only, not for value for money. As you will see in Chapter 8, total quality management is concerned with money.

Inspection, measuring and test equipment (4.11)

Test equipment in training and education 1

This section of BS 5750 appears to be only concerned with equipment used to demonstrate conformance of the product to specification. At first glance there appears to be no such equipment except that used by learners as part of the learning process. I will discuss that equipment shortly under the heading Test equipment in training and education 2.

Closer inspection reveals that this section has another important but subtle interpretation for training and education. The critical wording is in 4.11 (a) which states that the supplier shall:

identify the measurement to be made, the accuracy required and select the appropriate inspection, measuring and test equipment.

Since this is all to be done in order to 'demonstrate the performance of the product to the specified requirements', the meaning in training and education begins to emerge. It is referring to any instrument which training and education uses to ensure that the planned learning is taking place. Thus, the 'equipment' which is covered by this section might include:

81

- assessment materials;
- moderation systems;
- external examining systems;
- external awarding systems.

In plain language, section 4.11 is asking:

- How do you know that your test methods are measuring what you say they measure?
- How do you know that the measurements which you are taking on this year's course are using the same measuring system as last year's course?
- How do you know that measurements which you make are comparable with those made by another centre?

Or, as training and education would put it, testing has to be valid and reliable. As a reminder:

- Valid means that a test measures what we say it measures and not something else.
- Reliable means that if we give the same test on different occasions to different learners with the same performance level, we will get the same score.

Application of test equipment

The application is very straightforward in theory and near to impossible in practice. You will be all too familiar with the endless controversy which assessment produces in training and education. Rarely is there widespread or long-lasting agreement on how any particular item of performance should be tested. But BS 5750 is not an unreasonable master. You are not expected to take steps beyond those that are customarily accepted by your sector. If, for example, you work in a sector where external examining is the accepted means of standardizing marks, then you can continue to use that approach, provided that your customers are happy.

Test instrument	Validity checks	Reliability checks
Selection test	Standard test	Standard test
End of course award	National qualification (NVQ)	National qualification (NVQ)

Table 3.6 *Applying standardization of tests*

To apply this section then, you need to identify the critical systems which you use to check learner progress and make sure that you have taken proper steps to ensure their validity and reliability. Now this may sound as though you and your colleagues are about to become specialists in the technicalities of test design. That is unlikely to be the case. For most of your testing you will be relying on tests produced by awarding bodies. You can assume that what they produce is valid and reliable. BS 5750 does not expect you to duplicate their work.

A useful way of implementing this section is to draw up a list of all your test items and note against each how validity and reliability are monitored. Table 3.6 shows examples from such a table.

The table neatly side-steps the whole problem: the organization only uses tests which have been developed and moderated elsewhere.

Test equipment in training and education 2

The second aspect of this section refers to the use of equipment by learners where its calibration is critical to the quality of the learning. Equipment which is likely to fall into this category includes:

- any test or measuring equipment used to conduct

Item	Calibration frequency	Standard
Chemical balances	6 months	Accurate to .001 g
Voltmeters	6 months	1% accuracy

Table 3.7 *Setting calibration standards*

experiments where a given degree of accuracy is required for successful learning, eg electrical meters, ECG machines;
- any equipment which is used in an assessment test where the calibration of that equipment can affect the learner's score, eg chemical balance.

What the section of BS 5750 requires you to do here is too technical to repeat in detail, but the principles are simple enough. You have to make sure that:

- you know what has to be calibrated for what;
- calibrations are carried out;
- records are kept.

Application

Here application is a very simple piece of record keeping and could take the following two-part form:

1 Set the standards
Draw up a list of which equipment has to be calibrated, how often, and to what standard. This master table would have to be available to everyone involved in calibration. A sample table is shown in Table 3.7.

Such a table would probably be designated as a work instruction.

2 Set up a record for each piece of equipment

Calibration record for balance No 23	
Calibrated in accordance with work instruction No XXX	
Date	**Signed**
3/1/92	John Smith
12/7/92	Mary Jones
5/1/93	Ann Green

Table 3.8 *A calibration record*

Once the standard is set, there needs to be a record for each piece of equipment where its calibration history can be found. Entries need to be signed by whoever is authorized in the relevant procedure or work instruction. Table 3.8 shows an excerpt from such a record.

Inspection and test status (4.12)

What is inspection and test status?

The process refers to knowing what tests have been applied to something and what the result was. The clichéd TV advertisement shows the man (usually) in the white coat who stamps 'Passed' on the car as it rolls off the assembly line. 'Passed' is its inspection and test status. Reality is, of course, more complex since the totality of components in a car will have undergone hundreds of tests, leaving a mass of test records in all the various sub-contracting firms.

Inspection and test status in training and education

What we are testing is the learner. BS 5750 does not require us to stamp 'Passed' on learners' foreheads, nor

85

probably to change our existing procedures. All it requires is that the learner's test status is recorded. It is, in the normal learner records.

Control of non-conforming product (4.13)

What is non-conforming product?

In manufacturing, the idea of non-conforming product is simple. It refers to anything which has been made or partly-made which has failed to meet the specification. For example, a casting where the metal has failed to fill the mould or a micro-chip where contamination has prevented the correct formation of part of a circuit.

As soon as an item of non-conforming product is found it has to be isolated from the conforming materials and labelled to prevent accidental use. In some cases, after repair or reworking it may become a conforming product.

Non-conforming product in training and education

On the whole this section has very little application in training and education except for those people who wish to describe learners as products. For them, non-conforming product includes learners who have failed assessments. Since I am not treating learners as products, this section would be limited to items used in teaching which are faulty. These could include:

- damaged or out of date books;
- teaching materials which do not fit the latest syllabus;
- assessment items that are incorrect or no longer applicable.

BS 5750 requires you to take appropriate steps to make

sure that such items are not inadvertently used for learning. Such steps might include:

- clearly labelling the items as 'out of date', '1990 syllabus only', etc;
- storing them in a separate location which again might be marked in some way, eg 'Non-current teaching materials'.

Corrective action (4.14)

What is corrective action?

Chapter 2 introduced the idea of corrective action: putting right things that have gone wrong. Its ultimate aim is to prevent non-conforming product being delivered. This is achieved through detecting non-compliances in the QA system. Corrective action:

- corrects the immediate non-compliance problem;
- examines the underlying cause of the non-compliance in order to prevent a further occurrence.

The concept of corrective action is at the heart of QA since, in addition to putting immediate problems right, corrective action can lead to amending procedures. It is part of the developmental nature of QA systems.

Corrective action in training and education

A non-compliance in training and education is the same as one in manufacturing. Your procedures specify exactly what needs to be done and the work instructions specify how the tasks are to be done. Through the auditing, discrepancies may be detected. These discrepancies require corrective action.

87

Dealing with non-compliances

BS 5750 requires you to specify a system for corrective action. Your system must state:

- how a non-compliance is to be investigated to prevent it happening again;
- how records will be scanned to detect patterns of non-compliance (eg why do learners from the local electronics company always do so much worse that the average?);
- how preventive action is to be initiated to avoid recurrence;
- how the corrective action system is monitored and recorded.

This last item is important – even the corrective action system is open to monitoring to make sure it does not fall below the standard which you set.

In designing all this, you are expected to bear in mind the consequences of a failure and take appropriate action. Exam papers getting lost is serious and needs immediate action; poor performance of one particular course might be investigated in depth only once a year.

Applying corrective action

Corrective action in training and education is no different from that in manufacturing since a corrective action system does not specify the precise things that could go wrong – this will have already been done in the earlier procedures.

For example, your process control procedure may specify that employers are to receive reports on their trainees once every three months. If, later, an employer complains that the reports have not been received, the *corrective action procedure* comes into play. The procedure would specify the general approach to corrective action including:

- who takes action;
- how quickly action must be taken;
- what records of the action must be made;
- who has to be informed of the non-compliance.

However, while the corrective action procedure should be as general as possible and leave all detail about specific areas of failure to their own procedures, it can help to consider where the failures are most likely to occur. In training and education they are:

Customer/learner complaints about

- non-delivery of parts of a course;
- the quality of the teaching;
- assessments.

Audit results revealing

- lapses in the course design process;
- failure to keep full learner records – especially of assessments.

Handling, storage, packing and delivery (4.15)

How this section is interpreted depends very much on what you decide is the product. If, as some organizations do, you include the learner in the product, then your section 4.15 can include the physical care (eg lodgings) of the learner. I shall discuss this section on the assumption that the learner is not the product.

Perhaps the best way of interpreting this section is to say, 'If the product is the process of learning and what is learnt, what do we have to handle, store, pack and deliver to do this?' In this spirit, I shall now discuss 4.15.

The 'what needs to be stored' has really been identified in

my discussion so far. Depending on the work of your organization, this could include:

- learning materials;
- tools and equipment;
- materials on which learners work (eg wood);
- assessment materials.

Applying the handling and storage section

Under this section you are required to establish, and then to document, proper systems for storing whatever needs to be stored. As usual, you decide what needs to be stored but, once that is agreed, the system must be written down and available to all those who need to know about it. The requirements of your system are very straightforward:

- the storage method/location must prevent damage or deterioration;
- storage areas must be appropriately secure (ie you would have a different level of security for photocopying paper than for exam papers);
- appropriate methods for logging materials in and out must exist. 'Appropriate' might sometimes mean 'none' – you decide what is appropriate;
- items are properly marked;
- items waiting to be checked before use should be separated from items ready for use.

The whole of this has to be treated with the usual caution. QA actions are only justified if what they control is critical to quality as perceived by the customer. Much of storage in training and education is not critical and does not therefore justify elaborate systems.

Quality records (4.16)

What are quality records?

BS 5750 defines this very neatly. 'Quality records shall be

maintained to demonstrate achievement of the required quality and the effective operation of the quality system' (BS 5750: Part 1: 1987, section 4.16). In other words, quality records are whatever you have to keep in order to show that your system is working to plan.

Through having a special name like 'quality records' an unfortunate misconception readily arises: the idea that quality records are special records kept for the QA system and for no other reason. Where that is the case – and it does happen in some QA systems – then it's a very poor QA system. In a well-designed QA system, ordinary day-to-day records are planned in such a way as to be suitable as quality records.

What is special about a quality record?

If quality records should be ordinary records wherever possible, aren't all records quality records? The answer is 'No'. A record is only a quality record when it satisfies two criteria:

1 The requirement to keep the record is specified in a procedure.
2 The record meets certain requirements for labelling, retrievability and retention.

The requirements for labelling, etc are that the records shall:

• be legible;
• be identifiable with what they refer to;
• be easily retrieved when needed;
• have retention times specified.

This last point is perhaps the one which comes least naturally to people. When we first create a record, we rarely give a thought to when it should be destroyed. With quality records, specifying a retention period is essential in order to make sure that the records are not prematurely destroyed. It is important that the retention period is intelligently stated. For example, a procedure may say 'Assessment records are to be kept for two years from the date of the assessment'. That's fine. Copying that on to the actual file is useless since the date of the assessment may no longer be clear. Much better would be to label the file 'Keep until November 1994'.

Quality records in training and education

Deciding which records to keep as quality records is not easy and only the most general of guidelines can be given. The process starts as you write each procedure (see Chapter 4). As you check over each procedure, one thing which you have to check is the specification of the quality records. Asking two questions will help to minimize the record keeping:

- Can we manage without a record for this?
- If we really need a quality record for this, do we have an existing record which we can turn into a quality record?

While requirements will differ from organization to organization, almost all will have to keep as quality records:

- learner records, especially of courses taken, tests taken and results obtained;
- staff records, especially those which show qualifications held, appraisals and development activities;
- course design records and evidence of how they match market need.

Internal quality audits (4.17)

This is one of those sections where training and education practice does not differ from that in manufacturing. The requirement to set up a system which checks that your QA system is functioning as planned remains the same.

To comply with this section, you have to write a procedure which specifies how your organization is going to run its internal audit. The requirements that you have to meet are few but important. They are:

- to appoint internal auditors;
- to ensure that the auditors have the skills they need and to arrange training if needed;
- to have a schedule which ensures that the full range of procedures is audited.

Once the auditing procedure is in action, you will have to ensure that:

- audits are carried out to schedule;
- follow-up actions are carried out promptly;
- audit records are kept;
- audit progress is reported to those managing the QA process.

Frequency of audits

This is up to you, but BS 5750 does use the words 'on the basis of the status and importance of the activity'. Perhaps even more important is to consider the consequences of not auditing a particular area. What are the likely consequences of an undetected non-compliance in that area? The faster moving a process is and the more damaging a non-compliance can be, the more frequent the audits need to be. If this doesn't help, then you might start with auditing each section every six months and see how well that meets your organization's needs.

Choosing auditors

Few, if any, training and education organizations will have full-time auditors. For most, auditing only takes up a few days per year of each auditor. This means that auditors will be chosen from among your existing staff. All that BS 5750 has to say on this is that auditors must not audit their own work area – a sensible precaution.

Training (4.18)

This is another section where training and education are no different from manufacture. What BS 5750 requires is that *for those activities affecting quality*, only properly trained staff are used. This probably includes all of your staff since training and education is only deliverable through skilled staff. So, for staff in whatever areas or functions you decide are critical, you have to set up a procedure for:

- identifying the training needs of the staff;
- providing the training;
- keeping records of the training.

This does not mean that you will need to start carrying out extensive skills tests on all your staff. In training and education, almost all jobs are well defined, with clearly established standards or minimum qualifications. Eg a college may require all lecturers to have:

- a first degree or professional qualification in their subject;
- a further education teaching certificate.

If, in the opinion of the relevant managers, this is what is required for the job of lecturer, then records for each lecturer to show that they have these qualifications are sufficient to meet the BS 5750 requirement. Probably the best way to cover training is to write a procedure which says:

- X committee shall specify the qualifications for the following posts:

- trainer;
- senior trainer;
- lecturer, etc.
- For any other post, the manager responsible shall draw up a list of the skills required and check candidates against this list.

Servicing (4.19)

What is servicing?

Servicing refers to any contractually provided activity which takes place after the product has been made and delivered. We are fully familiar with this term in manufacturing: a video recorder under guarantee may be serviced by the manufacturer or the manufacturer's appointed agent.

Servicing in training and education

Few contracts to provide training or education include any commitment to provide after-course services. Occasionally a vocational training programme may include a review after the trainee has been back in work for, say, three months. Such a commitment would be 'servicing' in BS 5750 terms. Unless you are absolutely clear that your organization really does provide servicing of this type, it is best to ignore it when preparing your procedures.

Statistical techniques (4.20)

Section 4.20 is a very special reference to the use of statistical techniques, restricting its reference to techniques used for 'verifying the acceptability of process capability

95

and product characteristics'. It says that 'where appropriate', the supplier shall set up and use suitable statistical techniques. Can this ever apply in training and education?

In the strict process sense, the answer has to be 'No'. We do not use statistically-based process control charts which show us boundary values which we have to keep within. Given that the answer is 'No' in these terms, we have to go back to first principles and ask why 4.20 is there at all.

The point of 4.20 is to add a specialist piece of armoury to help decide whether or not the production is going to plan. In training and education, we too have to have adequate techniques to tell us whether we are achieving our objectives. Are learners learning what we said they would? If we can answer this question adequately without statistical methods, then fine. If we can only answer the question with the aid of statistical techniques, then we shall have to employ such techniques. In a nutshell, that is what 4.20 says.

As with 4.19, this is a section to ignore on a first implementation of BS 5750. If you find it really is necessary, then add it in later.

Summary

I do not intend to summarize this chapter in the straightforward sense. Instead, what follows is a list of the procedures which this chapter seems to indicate you are likely to need to write:

- Selection and counselling
- Course design (design control)
- Document control
- Purchasing and approved suppliers
- Teaching (process control)
- Assessment
- Testing supplies and equipment
- Auditing and corrective action
- Quality records
- Staff training.

Chapter 4

Writing Procedures

What is a procedure?

A procedure is a systematic statement describing how a particular function is to be carried out. Its purpose is to:

- define the work covered by the procedure;
- break the work down into discrete steps;
- define who is to carry out each step;
- define how work is passed from one step to the next.

The first decision that has to be made is to determine the scope of the procedure. In order to avoid having too many procedures, each covers a function which is large enough to have several, or even many, steps. Anything simpler than this is likely to be part of a procedure or the whole of a work instruction. How much each procedure should encompass is entirely a matter for the users of that procedure: if they find a procedure unwieldy, they may wish to split it. If they find it trivial, they may wish to combine it with something else.

This is all best illustrated by taking a practical example. For the rest of this chapter, I shall discuss how to write procedures by building up a procedure on counselling and admissions for a hypothetical training centre.

The flowchart

A good procedure will be logical, clear and easy to implement. To some extent these requirements can be met by careful writing, but a procedure can only be as good as the agreed way of working. If the working practices are chaotic, vague or inefficient, a procedure will faithfully reflect this. For this reason, the first step in writing a procedure is to write a flowchart describing the function which the procedure will cover. The purpose of writing the flowchart is to:

- reveal flaws in the current system, eg gaps in the system or duplicated tasks;
- explore whether present practice is the most efficient way of proceeding;
- allow discussion of how to revise the current practice into a more suitable form.

At one level, the flowchart is simply a planning tool to help you write a good procedure, but the flowchart itself can become part of the procedure, acting as a visual summary of what has been agreed. Our example will demonstrate this.

Designing the flowchart

To write a flowchart, you need to set down each of the steps in the process. It is best to start with a rough list, not worrying too much about whether the order is right or not. For example:

- give student enrolment pack
- offer counselling
- counsel
- enrol.

Once you have the rough list, you can then begin to think in a more systematic way about each task. We need to be

Action	Output	Who	Next
Hand pack to enquirer. Note enquirer details. Offer counselling date.	Enquirer details. Counselling booking.	Reception staff.	Counsel *or* end.
Counsel.	Counselling record.	Admissions tutor.	Enrol *or* end.
Enrol.	Enrolment form.	Admissions tutor.	End.

Table 4.1 *Enrolment actions*

able to say, for each task:

- what the action is;
- what the output of the action is – this is a cast-iron way of deciding whether the action is complete or not;
- who does it;
- what happens next – this helps us draw the flowchart and to get the tasks in the right order.

In some cases, 'what happens next' could be more than one thing, so we have to watch out for these cases. Table 4.1 shows the rough list above expanded in this way.

When you compile a list in this format, you may well find that certain aspects of the procedure are unclear. For example, you may find that:

- the output of an action is undefined;
- who should carry out an action has never been agreed;
- certain 'nexts' are unclear.

In this example, the analysis immediately reveals a possible hole in the procedure where we might wish to improve it.

At two points, enquirers might end their application. This is inevitable and the procedure should make allowance for this. But should the admissions procedure also find out and record why these enquirers decided not to enrol? This could be useful information for future course planning and marketing. I have made the assumption that it would be a good idea to record this information, so in the full flowchart (Figure 4.2), these extra steps occur.

Drawing the flowchart

Flowcharts are a formal way of recording a set of action steps and decisions as to which step comes next. Various conventions exist for drawing flowcharts, but in choosing your design, you need to stick to something that your colleagues will be comfortable with. For the purposes of this book, I have chosen to use only the symbols shown in Figure 4.1.

Using these symbols, we can convert the table of actions into the flowchart shown in Figure 4.2.

Writing the procedure

Now that we have worked out the basic structure of the function covered by the procedure, we can begin to write the procedure down. (If you think you can write a procedure without first drawing a flowchart, you might try it. My own experience is that the written procedure quickly becomes verbose without the initial clarity of the flowchart.)

A procedure usually contains a number of fairly standard sections such as:

1 purpose
2 scope
3 responsibilities
4 definitions
5 references

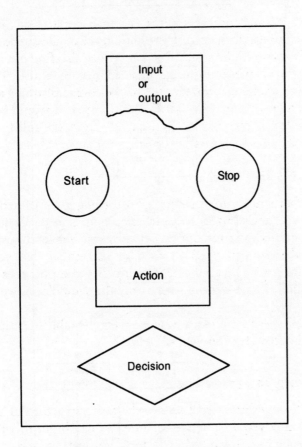

Figure 4.1 *Flow chart symbols*

6 the procedure detail
7 appendices.

It is easiest to follow the development of the sections if we start with the procedure detail.

Procedure detail

In the procedure detail we simply turn the flowchart into words, with one paragraph for each discrete step. For

101

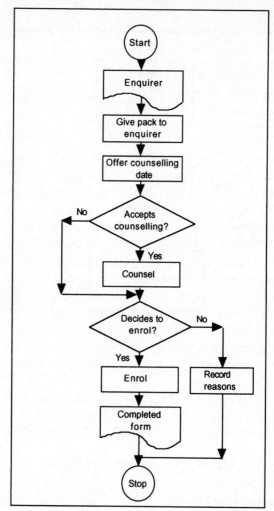

Figure 4.2 *A procedure flowchart*

example, take the step of handing the enrolment pack to the enquirer. This could be written as:

Reception staff shall handle initial enquirers, recording their names and addresses and handing (or sending) them a copy of the enrolment pack.

To test whether this is a good procedure statement, we must ask four questions of it.

- Does it include an action?
- Does it say who will do it?
- Does it say what the output will be?
- Is it auditable?

This paragraph satisfies all four questions. The action (there are two in this case) is 'record name and address' and 'hand over (or send) pack'. It is to be done by the reception staff. The output is the record of the name and address. Notice that the output cannot be 'hand over (or send) pack' since the enquirer leaves no evidence of having it. Since QA looks for evidence in the form of quality records, we have to structure procedure paragraphs in a way which creates a record of the completed action. In this case, the assumption is that all enquirers who have names and addresses recorded have been provided with the pack. Finally, we can audit this action by checking later that the QA record does hold the names and addresses – there is something physical to inspect.

As it happens, we find that our paragraph has defined its own quality record. To make this more explicit, we can, say, underline anything that is a quality record. The paragraph would then become:

Reception staff shall handle initial enquirers, recording their <u>names and addresses</u> and handing (or sending) them a copy of the enrolment pack.

Using this approach, the full body of the procedure can now be written. Since we need to be able to refer very precisely to paragraphs, each is numbered. The main body of the procedure is going to be section 6 (from the list of sections given earlier).

6.1 Reception staff shall handle initial enquirers, recording their names and addresses and handing (or sending) them a copy of the enrolment pack.

6.2 Reception staff shall offer each enquirer a counselling appointment with an admissions tutor. Such appointments shall be recorded in the counselling diary and assigned to one of the admissions tutors by the reception staff. The assignment shall be recorded in the counselling diary and the admissions tutor concerned shall be notified on form C3 by the reception staff. Admissions tutors must be given 48 hrs notice of appointments.

6.3 The admissions tutor shall counsel the enquirer and record any outcomes agreed with the learner on an admissions enquiry form.

6.4 If, at the counselling session, the learner definitely decides not to enrol, the admissions tutor shall record the reasons given by the learner on the admissions enquiry form.

6.5 If the enquirer completes an enrolment form at the counselling interview, the admissions tutor shall note the course(s) enrolled for on the admissions enquiry form. Completed enrolment forms and admissions enquiry forms shall be passed by the admissions tutor to the registry on the same day as they are completed.

You will recall that I said that each paragraph in the main part of a procedure should be checked to see:

- Does it include an action?
- Does it say who will do it?
- Does it say what the output will be?
- Is it auditable?

The above paragraphs have been phrased to meet these criteria. (The commonest errors in procedure writing are to

(a) forget to say who should do something ('Records shall be checked for . . .') and (b) to phrase it so that the output is unclear.)

In practice, a real working procedure is likely to have more paragraphs in the main section, but the additional paragraphs would be in the same vein as the examples above.

Now that we have the guts of the procedure, we can look at the other sections that will surround it. This time I will take them in order.

Purpose

This is usually a short paragraph which describes in non-technical terms what the procedure covers. Its purpose is to enable readers to decide whether they need to use the procedure at all or on a specific occasion.

For our example procedure, the purpose will be:

---

1 PURPOSE
1.1 The purpose of this procedure is to set out how enquirers are to be assisted in making decisions about whether to enrol with the centre.

Scope

The purpose is followed by a more formal scope section which enables a procedure user to determine the precise occasions on which the procedure is to be used. Quite often the scope section will list the occasions when it is not to be used.

The imaginary scope section for this procedure is:

---

2 SCOPE
2.1 The procedure shall be followed whenever an individual enquirer approaches the centre by letter, telephone or in person and asks either for details of courses on offer or for advice on a choice of course.

2.2 The procedure shall not be used when an employer or other sponsor approaches the centre about courses on offer. In such cases, the procedure on corporate enrolments shall be used.

Responsibilities

You have already seen that the body of the procedure says who is to do what so it may seem odd that a section on responsibilities is needed. There are two reasons why you might need this section.

First, in addition to the specific, task by task, definition of who does what, there may be overall responsibilities. They are listed here.

Second, to avoid long lists within the procedure body of who is to do which task, it may be useful to write the procedure more generally and then be specific in this section. For example, the hypothetical centre for this procedure might have no one with the title 'admissions tutor' but about seven different job roles who can do admissions counselling. It would have been awkward to say 'The course tutor, or the senior lecturer, or the head of department . . .'. The following responsibilities section deals with both these problems.

3 RESPONSIBILITIES

3.1 Overall responsibility for the admissions system and for the monitoring and revision of this procedure shall lie with the Senior Tutor (Admissions).

3.2 Any person who is requested by the Senior Tutor (Admissions) or by a Head of Department, to offer admissions counselling shall, for the purposes of this procedure, be termed an admissions counsellor.

3.3 Any person who is formally employed in the centre reception office or on the centre switchboard

shall, for the purposes of this procedure, be termed a
member of the reception staff.

Definitions

In this section you define any words in the procedure which
might have a special meaning within that procedure. Whether
something needs to be defined is a very local decision. Only
those who use a procedure know what is common knowledge
and what might need the clarification of a definition. Here I
have assumed that 'corporate enrolment' needs defining plus
the convention of underlining QA records.

> 4 DEFINITIONS
> **Corporate enrolment**: a corporate enrolment is one
> where the enrolment form is signed by the student's
> employer in the box 'corporate sponsor'.
>
> **Quality records**: the quality records for this pro-
> cedure are those items underlined in section 6.

References

Many procedures need to cross-refer to other procedures
or to work instructions. In order to keep procedures easy
to use, such cross-references should be kept to a minimum.
For this procedure, we shall have just two cross-references.

> 5 REFERENCES
> 5.1 **Corporate enrolment procedure**: refers to
> procedure number CEP010 Procedure on handling
> corporate enrolments.
> 5.2 **Admissions enquiry form**: refers to Form
> ADM105 Record of admissions enquiry – see
> Appendices.

As you can see, the references section is a useful way of enabling us to use shorthand titles within the body of a procedure without any loss of precision.

Procedure detail

This will be section 6. You have already met this above (p 101).

Appendices

Depending on their bulk, it may be useful to append key documents to the procedure. In this case, I have chosen to have just two appendices.

---

7 APPENDICES
7.1 Admissions enquiry form

[The actual form itself would then appear here.]

7.2 Flowchart

[The flowchart for the procedure would go here.]

The complete procedure

We now have a complete procedure. For clarity, this is reproduced as Appendix 1 to this book.

Who should write procedures?

So far I have assumed that you are going to write the procedures. In practice, this might not be the best way of proceeding. If QA systems are to work well, then the staff who have to put them into effect must feel that they have ownership of at least the parts that affect them. That in itself suggests that they will need to take responsibility for their own procedures. Additionally, only the staff who carry out a function know it well enough to write an accurate and workable procedure. It is therefore essential that procedures and their work instructions are written by those closest to where the work is done.

To write effective work instructions and procedures, individuals will need appropriate training which will need to cover:

- the principles of QA;
- quality records;
- the principles of auditing;
- flow charting;
- procedure writing;
- procedure testing.

This book does not go into the details of designing training programmes of this type but you will need to consider how such training is to be provided.

Checking a procedure

Even the most careful analysis and drafting is unlikely to produce a thoroughly workable procedure first time around. Equally, rounds of drafting and commenting may fail to pick up basic problems. There is, however, a method of checking procedures. It is called walk-through validation.

To validate in this way, you need to involve a person who is not too familiar with the function covered by the procedure. The validator's job is to:

- establish what is current practice;
- note the variations between current practice and the procedure's description of practice;
- look for tasks in current practice that are not in the

procedure – are they too trivial to include or too important to leave out?

- look for tasks in the procedure that are omitted in practice – should they be deleted from the procedure?
- ask the practitioners for their views on how the differences between current practice and the procedure should be resolved. Should the procedure be rewritten to reflect current practice?
- Should current practice change to reflect the procedure? Should both change?

With this remit, the validator sits down with one or more of the staff who carry out the function and asks them to describe exactly the steps in the jobs which they do. Using probing questions, the validator can help the procedure users to identify the discrepancies and decide what to do about them. The validator might ask questions like:

- You said that after you take the enquirer's name and address, you then file the record. Do you also offer a counselling appointment?
- You've just mentioned telephoning an admissions tutor to fix an appointment. How often do you do that rather than use form C3?
- And after that?
- And do you ever . . .?
- Do you find that's the best way to do it?

It is important that all those involved in the walk-through appreciate that they are not on trial about how they do their jobs. It's the procedure which is on trial. How well does it describe how the jobs are done?

It is not the validator's job to change the procedure but merely to help the procedure users recognize the gaps and discrepancies and to help them agree what changes are needed. This is made easier if the validator divides his or her work into distinct stages:

- identify without comment or discussion all discrepancies;
- discuss the discrepancies with the procedure users and establish a consensus on the precise nature of the discrepancies;
- discuss with the users what they wish to do about each discrepancy.

Distribution of procedures

Once the procedure is agreed to be an accurate reflection of how the function is to be carried out, it has to be circulated for use. Procedures are key documents, so their circulation has to ensure that:

- only accurate, authorized, copies are used;
- only up-to-date copies are used;
- no one who needs a copy is missed in the circulation.

To ensure that these requirements are met, procedures are issued through a system known as controlled circulation. This involves:

- maintaining a central list of those who need to use the procedure;
- when sending them a copy of the latest version of a procedure, asking them to return a signed slip confirming that they have (a) received the new version and (b) destroyed the old version.

This seems like a lot of work (it is), but all the effort of creating a QA system will be destroyed if staff dutifully follow the steps in out-of-date procedures.

Chapter 5

Writing Work Instructions

What is a work instruction?

You have seen in Chapter 4 how the main part of a procedure defines what needs to be done and by whom. It does not, however, tell the procedure user *how* to carry out the task. This may not matter. If the task is straightforward or the staff are fully trained before taking up the function, then an outline procedure may suffice. After all, the function of a QA system is to take reasonable steps to assure quality – not every conceivable step. The greater the consequences of error, the more prescriptive you have to be. If you do decide that you need to be more prescriptive than the detail in a procedure, you do this by providing additional work instructions which are used alongside the procedure.

A work instruction is therefore any additional mandatory guidance which accompanies a procedure.

What makes a good work instruction?

Convenient to handle

There is one very important difference between a procedure and a work instruction. On the whole, procedure users do not need to work with the procedure in front of them. Once they are fully aware of a procedure's contents, users will adjust their own working practices to ensure that they follow it. A procedure is not a job-aid. Work instructions, on the other hand, are best thought of as job-aids – something which is used as the job is done. This automatically gives us a requirement for a good work instruction: it should fit into the job as naturally as possible. For example, if you had a work instruction on preparing a training room for a training event, it would not be very convenient to place it in a heavy ring binder with dozens of other documents. The work instruction would be much more usable if it could fit on to a clip-board.

Follows the pattern of the job

Second, given that a work instruction is designed to tell someone how to do something, its format must follow the pattern of the job. To return to the training room preparation example, a convenient format for the work instruction would be a checklist of the items covered with an indication of what acceptable quality is.

Self-documenting

Third, it is convenient if work instructions are self-documenting. That is, if a quality record is needed for the application of the work instruction, then whatever recording needs to be done is best done on the work instruction itself. This makes the work instruction easier to use and increases the chances of the recording been done while not increasing the number of documents.

Self-explanatory

Fourth, work instructions should try to avoid references to other documents. The more self-contained a work instruction is, the easier it will be to use. Sometimes reference to another document is unavoidable, eg when completing registration forms, a person might have to refer to a prospectus or course list. The less this happens, the better.

An example work instruction

I shall now develop a work instruction for preparing a hypothetical training room. The need for this will have arisen from a procedure which will have referred to the work instruction. So, the procedure might have said:

> x.x Before each training event, the training assistant shall prepare the training room following work instruction W123.

We now have to write that work instruction.

If the task were complex, then it might be useful first to try and write a flowchart for it. In this case, it seems unlikely that the checks need to be made in any very strict order, so I will assume that a flowchart is not necessary.

Step 1 List all the tasks involved

Has trainer specified in writing:

– table positions?
– chair positions?
– A/V requirements?
Check is floor clean?
Are surfaces dust-free?
Are tables in specified positions?
Are chairs in specified positions?
Is A/V equipment in place?

OHP projector:

- plate and reflector clean?
- bulb working?
- spare bulb present?

Video monitor:

- channel correct?
- picture OK?
- sound OK?

Test video player:

- picture OK?

Step 2 Decide standards

It may be that you wish to lay down specific, measurable standards for certain tasks. For example, 'picture OK' is very subjective. You might decide to specify a certain level of picture resolution such as '4 MHz bars visible on test card'. So, the monitor entry would become:

Item	Standard
Video monitor:	
- channel correct?	n/a
- picture OK?	4 MHz bars visible
- sound OK?	n/a

Step 3 Convert to checklist format

If space is left for the user to record the outcome of each check, then the work instruction becomes its own quality record.

Item	Standard	Check	Comment
Video monitor:			
– channel correct?	n/a	☐	
– picture OK?	4 MHz bars visible	☐	
– sound OK?	n/a	☐	

Step 4 Add headings, etc

Once we have all the actions of the work instruction clear, we have to add the final touches. The work instruction will need:

- a title – which must exactly match that in the procedure;
- an edition number – to make sure that users do not use out-of-date editions;
- a note on when it is to be used;
- any instructions on how to use it;
- a space to record the signature and date of use;
- a note of where to file the completed work instruction or to whom it needs to be circulated.

The completed work instruction

Putting all these parts together, we get the completed work instruction which is shown in Appendix 2.

Other work instruction formats

The work instruction that we have just looked at was in checklist format. This is just one of many possible formats. In this section we shall look at some other formats for work instructions.

Algorithm

One of the many processes that you might wish to specify in

detail is a decision-making process. Frequently these are expressed as complex regulations or opaque prose. A much better way is to use an algorithm which then becomes a work instruction for the task. For example, Figure 5.1 shows an algorithm for implementing a particular assessment system.

A *standard*

Another type of work instruction is a standard to which work is expected to be done. As before, if we were to put the details of the standards into procedures, the procedures would become unwieldy. Instead, we use the procedure to refer to the standard. For example, a procedure might contain the paragraph:

x.x Each unit of learning material shall be checked by the editor who is responsible for ensuring that the standards set out in work instruction _____ are met.

Separately we would then write the standard, which might be something like the following:

WORK INSTRUCTION

STANDARDS FOR LEARNING MATERIALS

Objectives

The unit shall include learning objectives in behavioural form. Each objective shall include an action, a condition and a standard.

Learning activities

For each objective there shall be a sufficient range of learner activities to ensure that learners who meet the course pre-requisites have a 90% chance of mastering the objective within the unit study time.

Over a spread of units, a wide variety of activity

117

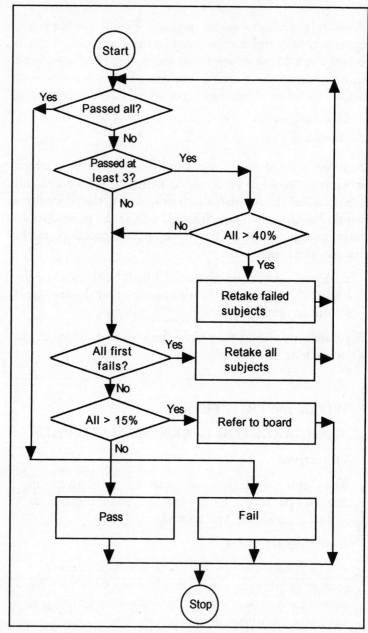

Figure 5.1 *An algorithmic work instruction*

methods shall be used. No one method should be used for more than 25% of activities.

Feedback shall be provided on each activity.

Self-assessment

For each objective, there shall be at least one self-assessment question.

All self-assessment questions shall have full answers.

Over a spread of units, a wide variety of self-assessment methods shall be used. No one method should be used for more than 25% of self-assessment items.

Language

Language shall be checked to ensure that it:
- is friendly
- is in the second person
- is non-sexist
- is non-racist
- uses short words in preference to long
- avoids the passive tense
- avoids over-complex sentences.

Notice that this is slightly different from the checklist example which I discussed earlier in this chapter. The checklist was highly prescriptive and the user was expected to work through every item on every occasion, recording the result in every case.

Here we have a standard which has to be applied when and where it proves necessary. It would be impossible to define in a standard exactly how many activities are needed in a piece of learning material. All that we can reasonably do is to set a standard in general terms which will be understood by the users of the work instruction.

Testing method

Any form of test which an organization uses in order to assure the quality of its work can be regarded as a work instruction since the test tells staff how to select or control a process. Selection tests (for staff and students), competence standards, psychological tests and so on might all be regarded as work instructions. On the whole, though, you are likely to wish to concentrate your QA activities on either (a) those tests which have the greatest potential to assure quality or (b) those tests which your organization has developed to meet its special needs.

The test does not have to be a set of questions – it could simply specify how a person is to be checked. Here is an example of a work instruction for selecting management tutors. As before, I first give the typical procedure paragraph that might point to this work instruction.

x.x The recruiting tutor shall select management tutors by the method set out in work instruction 333 Selection of Management Tutors.

WORK INSTRUCTION 333

SELECTION OF MANAGEMENT TUTORS

Applications

All applicants must complete the mandatory sections of the Tutor Application Form. Where any of these sections are blank, the form will be returned to the applicant.

Only applicants who meet the following criteria may be invited to the two day selection workshop.

Qualifications

Tutors must be selected only if they have the following qualifications:

120

– a management degree or diploma
– a teaching qualification.

Experience

Tutors must be selected only if they have the following experience:

– at least five years as a manager of at least five people
– at least two years experience as a trainer.

References

Tutors must be vouched for by two referees of whom at least one must be from their current employer.

Form

Another method of creating a work instruction is to define an existing generally available form as a work instruction. This differs from the previous methods in that the form cannot be labelled as a work instruction. This may seem odd, but many well-designed forms specify how they are to be completed and so can be regarded not only as data collection mechanisms, but also as instructions. Nor, to be a work instruction, must a member of staff necessarily personally complete all the form. As long as a member of staff is responsible for seeing that the form is completed, then the form can act as its own work instruction.

An example of this is an enrolment form. This may well be mostly completed by the applicant, but as long as a member of staff checks the form, then it can be used as a work instruction to control the enrolment process. Figure 5.2 shows such a form with a sign-off box for the member of staff.

This example illustrates the importance of not creating special QA documents where existing documents can be brought within the QA system.

Name (BLOCK LETTERS)		Title	Date of birth (d-m-y)
Address			
Post code	Tel No (day)	Tel No (eve)	Company
Course code	Course title		Fee
Signed (applicant)		Signed (tutor)	

Figure 5.2 *An enrolment form*

Layout format

My final work instruction example is the use of a diagram to show how something should be done. In this case the page layout specification for a worksheet shown in Figure 5.3 is an ideal form of work instruction.

Who should write work instructions?

Exactly the same points which I made about writing procedures apply to writing work instructions but possibly more so. Work instructions prescribe *how* a task shall be

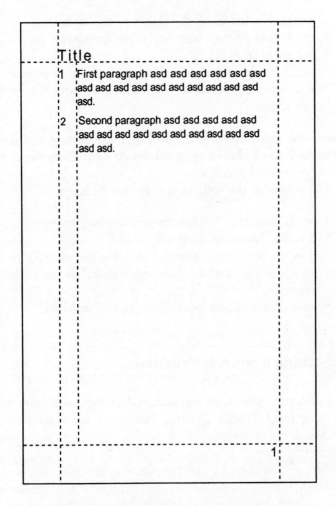

Figure 5.3 *Text layout as a work instruction*

done whereas procedures only describe what needs to be done. A work instruction which does not reflect how staff like to carry out a task will soon be discarded. It is therefore important that the people who will use a work instruction are involved in its writing.

The steps involved in this are to:

- establish a list of all the stages in the task;
- check that all the stages are really necessary;
- put them in order;
- ask: how do you know when this stage is complete?
- ask: how do you know when you have done this stage correctly?

For some staff, this analysis will be quite strange and they may well need skilled questioning to help them describe their own good practice.

Questions of the following type can be helpful:

- when you do . . . what do you do, step by step?
- do you always do *all* those things?
- how do you know when to vary the list of tasks?
- how do you know when each task has been done properly?
- how do you know when each task is finished?

Checking a work instruction

As with procedures, no amount of drafting can guarantee a perfect result. After drafting seems to have reached a reasonable consensus, the time has come to do walk-through tests.

This is best done by two people: one, the operator, to do the task and one, the observer, to check what is being done. The person doing the task does *not* have a copy of the work instruction during the walk-through; the observer does.

The operator performs the task as he or she would normally. The observer notes:

- tasks done exactly as described in the work instruction;
- tasks listed in the work instruction but not carried out;
- tasks not listed in the work instruction but carried out on this occasion;

124

- any variation between the operator's task order and the work instruction order.

Once the task is completed, the observer then takes the operator through all the variations. The two should try to identify which of the operator's variations require a re-wording of the work instruction and which do not.

This walk-through process should be repeated until no further significant variations occur.

Distribution of work instructions

These are distributed in the same way as procedures, described at the end of the previous chapter.

Chapter 6

Internal Auditing

What is internal auditing?

You have seen how a QA system differs from a quality control system. QA puts its emphasis on *assurance* of quality, rather than on tracing past mistakes. If a QA system is working well, its procedures and quality records will ensure that most work is done in the agreed manner and to the agreed quality. Having said that, management cannot sit back and assume that all will be well. There has to be a system for checking on the adherence to procedures and for dealing with any non-compliances that are found. This system is called *internal auditing*.

Internal auditing tends to go on throughout the year whereas most of this chapter will deal with carrying out a single audit. To avoid confusion, I shall call the total internal auditing activity of an organisation the *annual audit plan* but a specific audit will be called an *audit*.

A single audit involves checking on the workings of one procedure in one part of the organization. Thus the following might be single audits:

- audit of admissions procedure at site A;
- audit of approved suppliers procedure at department B;
- audit of assessment procedure at department C.

An annual audit plan is a timetable of all these separate audits.

What is the purpose of auditing?

In its simplest terms, the purpose of internal auditing is to *detect non-compliances to procedures*. It is useful to remember this phrase whenever an audit seems to be straying from its agenda. Inexperienced auditors and auditees can easily find themselves discussing, or even arguing about, many non-audit items. In each case, the question 'Is this part of detecting non-compliance?' will decide the issue.

However, the phrase 'detecting non-compliance' is very negative sounding, so we also need to think of internal auditing in a more positive sense. Put more positively, internal auditing:

- assures staff that they are following agreed systems;
- helps staff identify areas of uncertainty in procedures and work instructions and to agree clarifications;
- helps staff agree how non-compliances can be rectified;
- helps staff agree how procedures can be improved;
- helps management identify areas where all is well and areas where additional support is needed.

Despite these positive outcomes of auditing, staff may well feel threatened by the process. One reason for such fears is a simple but common misunderstanding: staff often presume that *they* are being audited. This is not the case. It is the *procedure* which is audited. Appraising staff or allocating blame for past problems is not part of auditing.

The annual audit plan

BS 5750 requires the organization to have an audit plan. This must demonstrate that:

127

Site	Procedure	Date	Auditor
South annexe	Admissions	June	A Smith
North annexe	Assessment	April	B Jones
Main site	Staff training	Sept	C Green

Table 6.1 *Part of an annual audit plan*

- all relevant sections (eg sites, departments) are covered;
- all procedures are covered;
- procedures or sites that are known to be weakest receive the heaviest audit attention.

This last point is important. Auditing is meant to be sensibly applied as a key management tool. If your organization runs 90% of its courses at site A and 10% at site B, the vast majority of the audit effort should be at site A. Similarly, if the bulk of past non-compliances or customer complaints have been about, say, the quality of your tutors, then the bulk of the audit resource will be around the relevant procedures such as staff selection and training.

The annual audit plan itself should be a simple document showing:

- the site/section to be audited;
- the procedure(s) to be audited;
- the audit date;
- the lead auditor.

An excerpt from an annual audit plan is shown in Table 6.1.

Notice that the plan only fixes the date to the nearest month. This leaves the auditor and the site staff to agree the precise day or days nearer the time. If you tie down audits

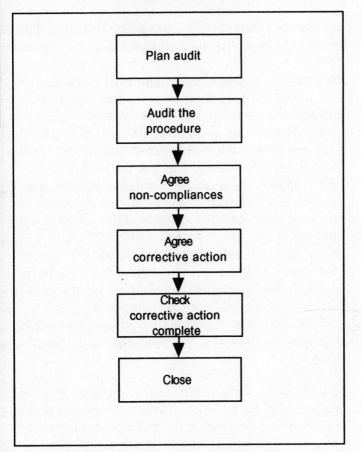

Figure 6.1 *The internal audit cycle*

more precisely than this, you will only find yourself having
to amend the schedule every other week.

The audit cycle

Every audit consists of a fixed cycle of activities. These are
illustrated in Figure 6.1.

I shall now work through this cycle in more detail by

reference to a hypothetical procedure. This procedure is assumed to contain the following clauses.

6.1 The assessment administrator shall ensure that all candidates for assessment are allocated an assessment number and that the number and candidate's name are entered into the assessment record by the administrator. The assessment administrator shall hand a copy of the Competence Assessment Guide to the candidate.

6.2 The assessment administrator shall allocate to the candidate an assessor from the Approved Assessors List and shall note this in the candidate's assessment record.

6.3 After each assessment, the assessor shall record the result and date in the candidate's assessment record. The result shall be recorded as one of 'C' (competent) or 'NC' (not yet competent).

6.4 As each piece of evidence is seen and approved by the assessor, the assessor shall sign and date the evidence.

6.5 When a candidate has completed the full qualification, the assessor shall compile a list (two copies) of all the evidence and place the list plus all the evidence in a verification file and pass this file to the internal verifier. The internal verifier shall sign one copy of the list of evidence and hand it to the assessor as a receipt for the folder.

(Underlined items are quality records.)

I shall now work through how such a procedure might be audited.

Step 1: *Prepare the checklist*

First the auditor needs to decide what evidence needs to be looked for and to put this into the form of a checklist for

Clause No.	Requirements	Compli- ance?	Comments
6.1	All candidates have assessment numbers and names in the assessment record.		
6.2	Assessor allocated to each candidate.		
6.2	Assessor is on approved list.		
6.3	Competences recorded as N or NC with date.		
6.4	Evidence signed and dated.		
6.5	Verifiers have verification files.		
6.5	Assessors have receipts for verification files.		

Table 6.2 *An audit checklist*

the actual audit. Table 6.2 illustrates a checklist for this procedure.

The first two columns of Table 6.2 are a careful analysis of the evidence which the procedure requires staff to keep. The compilation of this checklist is very important since (a) auditors need to be certain that they understand what it is they are about to audit and (b) they must be sure that they do not enquire about practices not required by the procedure.

Columns (3) and (4) are for use during the audit itself, so I will discuss those at the relevant step.

Step 2: The introduction

This will take place at a time mutually convenient to the auditor and auditee. Since it is the procedure that is being audited, not the auditee, the auditee can be anyone in the relevant section who is able to provide access to all the records and knows how they are used. Practice varies as to whether the audit checklist should have been sent in advance. I favour the checklist being sent in advance since I consider the whole QA system should be seen as one in which everyone is working together to maintain and improve the organization's standards. There is no 'them and us' in QA.

The audit starts with introductions and agenda setting and will normally include the auditor clarifying the proposed audit procedure. This should include:

- stating which procedure is to be audited;
- asking the auditee to confirm that he/she is the right person for this procedure;
- producing (if not sent in advance) the checklist and explaining what is being looked for;
- explaining that the auditor's role is to agree with the auditee any non-compliances and to record those in writing;
- also, but sometimes after the audit meeting, to agree corrective actions for each non-compliance.

Step 3: Working through the checklist

The auditor introduces each item on the checklist and asks the auditee to show him/her the evidence that the clause has been complied with. In almost all circumstances, only a tiny fraction of cases can be considered. For instance, in the case of my assessment example, the centre might have carried out 2000 assessments but the auditor might have time to check only five. It is important that the auditor chooses an appropriate sampling method. 'Appropriate' means a method which is likely to select typical cases. In the assessment procedure example, the auditor might select cases to audit by asking to see:

- all assessments registered on a particular day;
- every 100th assessment, starting with the first on the record and then working sequentially through every 100th;
- every 100th selected using a random number table.

Whatever method is used, the one thing the auditor must not do is to allow the auditee to suggest which cases to look at.

Having decided on the sample, the auditor then works through the checklist for each case. The auditor's main role at this stage of the audit is to determine whether to enter 'Yes' or 'No' in the compliance column of Table 6.2. The auditor is not permitted to enter anything else in this column. Compliance is an all-or-nothing process. You are not allowed to record '75% compliance' or 'just about' or 'looks like it' or anything else which is not clear cut.

Having entered 'Yes' or 'No' under compliance, you may wish to add an *aide mémoire* in the comments column, eg 'No date'.

I shall now assume that the auditor and auditee have completed this step, and the auditor checklist for two of the cases examined now look like Tables 6.3 and 6.4.

Step 4: Agree non-compliances

Wherever possible, auditors try to ensure that there is no disagreement about the facts of their reports. It is therefore important that the auditor takes the auditee through each of the non-compliances as he/she sees them and agrees on a wording to record these. At this stage, neither party should be concerned about why a non-compliance might have occurred. I shall assume that my auditor and auditee were able to agree on the facts and that they recorded the non-compliances in the format in Table 6.5.

If the auditor has spotted a serious non-compliance, he/she might ask to look at more cases. What is 'serious' is a

Clause No.	Requirements	Compli-ance?	Comments
6.1	All candidates have assessment numbers and names in the assessment record.	Yes	
6.2	Assessor allocated to each candidate.	Yes	
6.2	Assessor is on approved list.	No	
6.3	Competences recorded as N or NC with date.	No	Dates missing
6.4	Evidence signed and dated.	Yes	
6.5	Verifiers have verification files.	Yes	
6.5	Assessors have receipts for verification files.	Yes	

Table 6.3 *The audit checklist for candidate 90*

matter of opinion, although 'serious' must mean that the non-compliance has important implications for quality as perceived by the customer. In Table 6.5, the serious non-compliance is probably the use of an assessor who is not on the approved list. The use of such an assessor might invalidate the assessments so that they all have to be done again. In these circumstances, the auditor would be fully justified in looking at a larger sample of assessments to see if there has been repeated use of non-approved assessors.

Step 5: Make out corrective action requests (CARs)

This is the start of the most important part of QA: putting right non-compliances and taking action to prevent the problem recurring. For each non-compliance, the auditor makes out a CAR. This formally asks the auditee:

Clause No.	Requirements	Compliance?	Comments
6.1	All candidates have assessment numbers and names in the assessment record.	Yes	
6.2	Assessor allocated to each candidate.	Yes	
6.2	Assessor is on approved list.	Yes	
6.3	Competences recorded as N or NC with date.	Yes	
6.4	Evidence signed and dated.	No	Signatures missing
6.5	Verifiers have verification files.	Yes	
6.5	Assessors have receipts for verification files.	No	

Table 6.4 *The audit checklist for candidate 120*

1 to take note of the non-compliance;
2 to propose what action will be taken to put the particular non-compliance right;
3 to propose what action will be taken to prevent reccurrence of the problem;
4 to agree a date by which the corrective action will be complete.

Not every non-compliance justifies action to prevent recurrence. Where the auditor and auditee agree that no such action is required, then they can simply record the preventive action as 'None needed'.

Only the first part of the CAR action list has to be completed at the time of the audit. This is to prevent any risk of the parties disagreeing about the non-compliances

Audit of Assessment Procedure at site A, 10 May 1992 Record of non-compliances	
Clause No	**Non-compliance**
6.2	Mr X, not on approved assessor list, used as assessor
6.3	Some competences recorded without dates
6.4	Some evidence not signed by assessor
6.5	Some assessors do not have receipts for verification files handed to verifiers

Table 6.5 *A record of non-compliances*

after the audit meeting has finished. Items (2) to (4) may have to be left for a few days. For example, the auditee may have to discuss with colleagues what action is to be taken. For the purposes of this example, I shall assume that auditor and auditee did agree on all the corrective actions. A sample of how one such CAR would be recorded is shown in Table 6.6.

At this point the audit meeting closes but the audit itself is not finished. The remaining stages, discussed below, could go on for weeks. As you can see, the final section of the CAR form has not been completed except for setting a target date for full completion (closure) of the audit. The rest of this last section of the form is space for a record of progress on corrective action.

Step 6: Follow-up action

On the appointed date for completion of the corrective action (10 June 1992 in the above example), the auditor will revisit the auditee to check on progress on the cor-

136

CORRECTIVE ACTION REQUEST		Audit date 10 May 1992
Auditor A Smith	**Auditee** B Jones	**Audit site** Site A
Non-compliance Non-approved assessor used for candidate 90. **Signed (auditor)** A Smith **Signed (auditee)** B Jones		
Corrective action proposed Candidate 90's work to be re-marked by approved assessor. **Signed (auditor)** A Smith **Signed (auditee)** B Jones		
Prevention of further occurrence		
Approved assessor list to be kept with assessment record. Approved assessor list to be recirculated to all assessment administrators. **Signed (auditor)** A Smith **Signed (auditee)** B Jones		
CAR closure **Target date for closure** 10 June 1992 **Record of audit follow-up** **CAR closure date** **Signed (auditor)**		

Table 6.6 *A Corrective Action Request*

rective action. Assuming that all the agreed actions have been taken, the auditor completes the final section of the CAR and formally declares the CAR closed. This is shown in Table 6.7.

The CAR is closed, that is, it is finished with.

CAR closure

Target date for closure 10 June 1992

Record of audit follow-up
Re-assessment of candidate 90 had been completed by H Brown –
an approved assessor.
Assessor list is now with the assessment record.
Memo plus the assessor list circulated to relevant staff.

CAR closure date 10 June 1992
Signed (auditor) A Smith

Table 6.7 *The finally completed CAR*

Failure to complete CARs

In my example, I have assumed ready agreement of auditor
and auditee on the non-compliances and on suitable corrective action. I have also assumed that the work area being
audited sorts out the corrective action by the agreed
deadline. When this does not happen, more serious action
may be required. In the worst cases, if a section fails to sort
out non-compliances so that a CAR cannot be closed, the
auditor can issue a special CAR for failure to comply with
the QA system itself. It's just like being fined for a minor
offence by a court and, not having paid the fine, finding
yourself up for the more serious offence of failing to pay
the fine. Any organization which tolerates non-action on
CARs is permitting the total undermining of its QA
system, so most organizations treat it as a matter of great
importance to management.

Step 7: Close the audit

The audit itself cannot be closed until every CAR arising
from it has been closed. In the example which I am

following, there were four non-compliances so there will be four CARs. So far, one CAR is closed and three are outstanding. For brevity's sake, I shall not pursue the other three CARs.

Step 8: Follow-up audit

Sometimes an auditor finds such serious or multitudinous non-compliances as to require much more intensive auditing of the section. In such cases, most QA systems would require the auditor to fix a further audit in the near future, well ahead of the next routine audit in the annual plan. This is a good demonstration of how auditing capacity is directed to wherever the most serious quality problems are.

Do's and don'ts of auditing

Auditing is a very skilled activity – I shall say something about training for it shortly – requiring a special combination of personal qualities, perception and objectivity. In this section, I touch on some of the human aspects of auditing.

Audit the procedure, not the person

I have emphasized this point before, but repeat it here because of its personal qualities implications. Management is full of occasions when we have to focus on the task, not the person. Some managers have the necessary objectivity to make the distinction; others do not. No one should be trusted with an audit if there is any doubt about his/her capacity to remain non-judgmental about the auditee.

Open and closed questions

Skilful use of open and closed questions is required in auditing, taking great care not to lead the auditee.

First, the auditor has to establish at a factual level how the procedure has been applied to each case in the sample. So, referring to the assessment procedure example, the auditor might use questions such as:

- Can you show me the assessment record for candidate 90?
  (Auditee produces relevant record of assessment record.)

- I am not sure which of these items is the candidate's number. Can you tell me which it is?
  (Auditee points to the number in the record.)

- How can you tell to which assessor candidate 90 has been allocated?
  (Auditee names the assessor and shows assessor's name in the record.)

- According to clause 6.2, the assessor has to be chosen from the approved list. Can you show me your approved list and where Mr X appears on it?

This form of questioning makes clear what type of information is required, but tests whether the auditee can find the relevant information from the records. This is not, as might appear, a test of the auditee, but a test of the adequacy of the records.

Later, in order to pin details down more precisely, closed questions might be needed, such as:

- So, do I understand that you cannot find Mr X on the approved assessor list?
  (Requires a yes or no answer.)

- How many records do you think seem to be missing from this file?
  (Requires an estimated number.)

Throughout the audit, the aim is to remain friendly and

supportive but to ensure that the answers are the auditee's unprompted, honest view as to the facts. If the audit results become coloured by the auditor's views, then the audit will have failed to achieve its purpose.

Objectivity

In addition to the necessity for objectivity over the separation of the procedure and the auditee, a generally objective, non-judgmental, approach is needed throughout the audit.

In most organizations, auditing is an odd job done by members of staff with other full-time commitments. While the auditor must be independent of the section being audited (so, say, admissions cannot audit itself), inevitably the auditor is part of the organization and its politics and rivalries. All these have to be set aside during the role of auditing.

Avoiding discussion

It is not the auditor's job to discuss or argue with the auditee. In particular, the auditor must be on the look-out against being drawn into political or management arguments. 'I know quality records are a mess but look at what management's done to us in the last six months. There was all that fuss about budget cutbacks, then the reorganization . . . You can't keep to the QA system under those circumstances, can you?' The good auditor will diplomatically deflect this and return to the objective agenda.

Sometimes the stricture on no arguing requires the auditor to agree to differ. Suppose, in the assessment example, that the auditee had maintained that, despite not being on the approved list, Mr X was an approved assessor, then instead of arguing, the auditor would say, 'I am recording that you consider Mr X to be an approved assessor and that I, having looked at the approved list, am unable to find his name on that list.'

141

Maintaining confidentiality

While auditing is not about people, but about systems, auditees and their colleagues are still likely to be sensitive about any non-compliances found in their areas. Additionally, some of the records that an auditor needs to look at may be personal or confidential. Auditors must therefore be capable of maintaining confidentiality. Once your auditors cease to be trusted, your auditees will cease to reveal all.

Auditor selection and training

BS 5750 requires that auditors do not audit the areas within which they work. Equally, it helps if auditors understand what they are auditing. This means that you need to select auditors who are as close to the work to be audited as possible, without breaching the BS 5750 requirement for independence.

Once auditors have been selected, they need to be trained. Fewer than two days of training will leave auditors very light on the skills they need; typically, two days' initial training and a top up of one to two days after a few months' experience is desirable.

The training programme itself will need to cover:

- the principles of QA, procedures and quality records;
- devising checklists from procedures;
- identifying compliance and non-compliance;
- preparing CARs;
- tracing corrective action;
- closing CARs and audits;
- techniques of questioning;
- handling difficult auditees.

Chapter 7

Management Responsibilities

Introduction

Section 4.1 of BS 5750 Part 1 sets out the role of management in a QA system. There are three main elements to this: setting the quality policy; organizing the quality system; and reviewing the quality system. This chapter sets out how that can be done in a training or education organization.

Quality policy

General principles

You have already seen that idealistic and vague phrases such as 'to the highest possible quality' have no place in a QA system. You have also seen how, through the detailed analysis and precise wording of procedures, quality can be assured in a practical way. A quality policy lies somewhere between these two extremes. It must not be so vague as to be anodyne, nor must it be so detailed as to overlap the procedures.

In phrasing a quality policy, it helps to keep in mind its audience. Whereas procedures are written at the specialist level, with each member of staff using only one or two

143

procedures, the quality policy is common to all staff. It must therefore be written in terms which make it understandable without specialist knowledge of any particular training function and it must be relevant to the work of all employees.

In addition to keeping in mind the quality policy's audience, an awareness of its purpose helps as well. BS 5750 states that management has to ensure that the 'policy is understood, implemented and maintained at all levels in the organization' (BS 5750: Part 1: 1987, 4.1.1). In the context of training and education organizations, 'at all levels' includes part-time teachers, lecturers and non-teaching staff. These latter categories are a useful touchstone for writing the quality policy. What do they need to know about the principles of the quality system if they are to do their jobs effectively?

Quality policy contents

No fixed content for the policy is prescribed by BS 5750 but your assessors will take some convincing if your policy does not include:

- your organization's mission;
- a description of the management system for QA;
- the general responsibilities of staff for QA;
- how QA is documented;
- the range of functions for which you have procedures;
- how management review operates.

A typical quality policy is set out below.

____ TRAINING CENTRE QUALITY POLICY

Mission

____ training centre exists to provide high quality management development programmes. It aims to ensure that it is always regarded by its customers as the leading supplier in the area.

144

Quality commitment

_____ training centre is committed to providing a high quality service to its customers. As part of that service, the centre has implemented a quality assurance (QA) programme. The centre management regard the QA programme as the primary means of meeting its mission and targets.

QA management

The QA system is the responsibility of the QA Management Review Group, chaired by the centre's Chief Executive. This group is responsible for all QA policy decisions and for monitoring the effectiveness of the QA system.

Day-to-day operational management of the QA system is the responsibility of the QA Manager. The QA Manager oversees the introduction of all new procedures, runs the audit programme, monitors the running of the QA system and reports to the Management Review Group.

Staff responsibilities

Individual members of staff are responsible for implementing the QA system within their own work areas. In particular, they should:

- ensure that they have up-to-date QA documentation;
- familiarize themselves with the documentation;
- carry out work in accordance with the QA procedures and work instructions, maintaining quality records as required.

The overall aim of the QA system is to meet customers' requirements. If at any time a member of staff believes that there is a conflict between the customer's requirement and the QA procedures, he/she should

145

first meet the customer's requirement and then report the discrepancy to the QA Manager. **At no time should the QA system be implemented in a manner which is detrimental to the customer.**

QA documentation

In addition to this quality policy, the QA documentation includes:

* the procedures manual, one copy of which is held by each centre department;
* work instructions which are distributed to the relevant members of staff.

Functions with QA procedures

Procedures are provided for:

* Selection and counselling;
* Course design;
* Document control;
* Purchasing and approved suppliers;
* Teaching;
* Assessment;
* Checking supplies and equipment;
* Auditing and corrective action;
* Quality records;
* Staff training;

Management review

The Management Review Group shall review the QA system every six months and in particular shall monitor: adherence to the audit programme, the level of non-compliances and the promptness of corrective action. Where the QA programme is found to be ineffective or failing to meet customers' needs, the Management Review Group shall initiate appropriate changes to the system.

The quality system

It is unrealistic and inappropriate for the Management Review Group, or even the QA Manager, to carry out all the detailed work on the QA system. Equally, the tasks cannot just be left for anyone to pick up at whim. What is needed is a clearly defined system with responsibilities and reporting lines. BS 5750: Part 1, para 4.1.2.1 sets out a number of required responsibilities. This paragraph of BS 5750 can give the impression that you should establish a new set of responsibilities apart from your organization's job descriptions. That is not the case. What you do need to do is to ensure that *existing* job descriptions include necessary QA responsibilities. I shall consider how to implement this in two stages: (a) QA system responsibilities and (b) service-specific QA responsibilities.

QA system responsibilities

When you introduce a QA system, certain new tasks and responsibilities come with it. These will not be in the existing job descriptions of your staff so those job descriptions will have to be amended. First, you will need to identify what the new tasks are. These are likely to be:

- setting and revising QA policy;
- monitoring QA policy and implementation;
- selecting and training procedure writers;
- selecting and training work instruction writers;
- selecting and training auditors;
- setting and monitoring the audit schedule;
- preparing QA monitoring reports for the Management Review Group.

Once you have your list of tasks, these will need to be assigned to the relevant members of staff through your normal negotiating channels for agreeing job descriptions. These job descriptions then become part of your QA system and an external assessor will expect to see them in order to check that QA tasks have been clearly and fully allocated.

Service-specific responsibilities

Although you may have one person with a central role to train procedure and work instruction writers, no central person can have enough local knowledge to know what should be in a procedure or to detect when a procedure needs revision. All this detailed QA implementation has to be added in to job descriptions at the most local level possible. The tasks to delegate in this way include:

- writing procedures;
- circulation of procedures;
- keeping procedures under review;
- writing work instructions;
- circulation of work instructions;
- keeping work instructions under review;
- maintaining quality records.

One way of doing this is to nominate a *procedure owner* for each procedure, leaving that owner to carry out or delegate the tasks associated with the procedure. If this is your approach, then you will need two key QA system documents: the list of procedure owners and the procedure owners' responsibilities. Examples of such documents are set out in Figures 7.1 and 7.2.

The Quality Manager

You will almost certainly need to appoint one person to have overall day-to-day management of the QA system. In a small organization, this will not be a full time job and the

PROCEDURE OWNERS	
Course design	A B Smith
Document control	C D Green
etc	

Figure 7.1 *Sample list of procedure owners*

PROCEDURE OWNERS' RESPONSIBILITIES

1 To write procedures as assigned.
2 To keep their procedures under review and to make revisions as necessary to continue to meet customers' requirements.
3 To circulate procedures to those members of staff who need them and to ensure that all out of date issues are withdrawn from use.
4 To appoint work instruction authors for those work instructions specified in their procedures.
5 To circulate work instructions to those members of staff who need them and to ensure that all out of date issues are withdrawn from use.
6 To advise the Management Review Group through the QA Manager of any additional initiatives (in the work area covered by the procedure) needed to ensure that the QA system meets customers' requirements.
7 To advise the Management Review Group through the QA Manager of any quality problem that cannot be remedied through the existing QA system.

Figure 7.2 *Procedure owners' responsibilities*

149

role might be taken on by a senior trainer, a head of department or some other person of authority within your organization. (If you appoint someone too low in the hierarchy, they will find it difficult to gain the attention they need from other colleagues.)

The role of the Quality Manager is to ensure that the decisions of the Management Review Group are implemented. A typical Quality Manager's job description will include the following tasks:

- preparing agendas and papers for the Management Review Group;
- preparing and issuing minutes of Management Review Group meetings;
- liaison with the external QA assessor;
- setting the audit schedule;
- monitoring the audit schedule;
- identifying and providing for the QA training needs of staff.

Reviewing the system

The BS 5750 requirement

Para 4.1.3 of BS 5750: Part 1 requires that the system be reviewed at 'appropriate intervals . . . to ensure its continuing suitability and effectiveness'. Your external assessors will place great emphasis on this review system since it is tangible evidence of senior management commitment to QA.

Sorting the wood from the trees

It is all too easy to introduce a mechanical review system which checks that each QA task and process is being carried out. That has to be done, and I shall deal with that shortly. First, though, the review system needs to ensure that it is centred on the customer. Unless the Management Review Group knows what the customers' requirements are, they cannot ensure that the organization meets those requirements. Equally, unless adequate performance measures are in place, the Management Review Group cannot compare performance to another period or to customers' requirements. This suggests that the management review should focus on three major issues:

- What is the *latest* customer requirement?
- What is our *current* performance level?
- What does the QA audit record tell us?

I shall look at each of these in turn.

The customer requirement

The Management Review Group will need to check that adequate systems are in place to determine customer requirements and that the data from the systems is up to date. For example, data might come from:

- learner in-course feedback;
- learner end-of-course feedback;
- employer satisfaction surveys.

The primary emphasis here is on comparing need with what was delivered. Issues such as the following might be explored.

- Learner satisfaction with quality of the teaching, quality of teaching materials, premises, library facilities, pace of the course, degree of flexibility, assessment methods, value and relevance of the course content, value and relevance of the final qualification.
- Employer satisfaction with the course objectives, the

qualification, price, delivery times, pace, degree of employer involvement.

One does, however, need to keep a sense of proportion. Not every aspect of every course can be monitored in equal depth, so monitoring facilities need to be concentrated in areas where either most problems seem to be occurring or where the market is changing fastest.

Current performance level

In addition to collecting views on your organization's performance, the Management Review Group will need more objective measures of the results of the organization's work. These will include:

- internal course marks/grades;
- performance on external awards;
- jobs, promotion or further training gained by students after completing your courses.

In each case, it is particularly helpful to (a) express the figures in some comparative form (eg percentage of intake) and (b) to have longitudinal figures for a reasonable period of years or intakes. The absolute figures matter less than the trend. 'Are results improving?' is the crucial question for QA.

The QA record

Finally, we come to the QA record. It may seem odd to put it last after this book has spent so much time on showing you how to set up a QA system, but there is a good reason. QA monitors your *processes* (albeit through looking at intermediate outputs). It does this because, by the time you get the results, it is too late to put defective processes right. However, the processes are not what your organization is

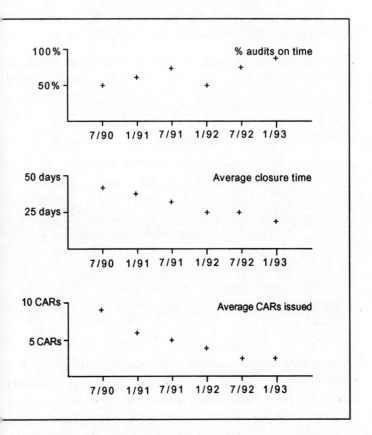

Figure 7.3 *Typical audit monitoring graphs*

there for. It is there to get results such as competences
gained, awards achieved, jobs obtained, and so on. It is
therefore essential to push the management review to first
consider the results and only then consider the processes.

The key part of the QA record is the audit record. First,
the Management Review Group must consider the
adequacy of the audit system with questions such as:

• Are we auditing enough locations?
• Are audits frequent enough?

153

- Are we using our audit resources wisely, concentrating them on areas of greatest non-compliance?

Second, the Group will need to ask questions about the audit record itself:

- What percentage of audits started on time?
- What is the average closure time?
- What is the average number of CARs raised?

However, the Group must remember that it is the trend that matters more than the absolute number and, for this reason, the QA Manager might find it useful to present the audit record in the form of a longitudinal record as in Figure 7.3. These particular examples show the kind of progressive improvement that a management review would be looking to see.

Management review outcomes

As with all evaluation, there is little point in having a management review system if actions do not follow where they are needed. The principle areas in which a Management Review Group might need to act are:

- reorientation of the organization to a new customer requirement;
- action to stem a fall in one or more performance standards;
- action to increase or change priorities in the audit schedule;
- action to produce new or revised procedures;
- further staff training in QA skills including auditing, procedure and work instruction writing.

Chapter 8

Towards Total Quality Management

Introduction

In Chapter 1, I referred to the distinction between quality control (QC) and quality assurance (QA). The latter has grown out of the former. Now we also have total quality management (TQM). In this chapter I will look at the similarities and differences between QA and TQM and discuss the relative merits of following the QA or TQM route.

TQM – an overview

The driving force behind TQM

TQM started its existence in those markets where Japan and the USA were in direct competition. It has continued to spread wherever markets are characterized by an ever increasing demand for quality and reliability combined with a fall in prices in real terms. Thus, TQM is particularly common in car manufacture and electronics, both areas where today's products are far more reliable than those of 10 to 20 years ago.

Training and education markets do not as yet experience competitive pressures of this type. However, as the worldwide privatization trend continues, it is likely that trainin and education will become more competitive. Particularl with the aid of high-tech media, customers will less and les turn automatically to their nearest local training or educa tion provider. It is therefore reasonable to hypothesize tha training and education providers will increasingly fin themselves competing on both quality and price. Th conditions for TQM could be on the way.

The philosophy of TQM

TQM works on the assumption that suppliers (in this case providers of training and education) will only survive ii their markets if they are able to both improve quality an reduce costs. While this notion is not novel in manufactur ing industry, it is perhaps revolutionary in training an education. We frequently read of teachers asking for mor resources so that they can improve quality. TQM says tha you must improve quality with fewer resources, because, i you don't, your competitor will.

That sounds tough – it probably is – but TQM assume that there is a hidden source of fat in any organization. Tha source is 'the cost of quality'. I use the term because that i what is standard throughout the TQM literature, but 'th cost of quality' is really 'the cost of non-quality', ie th money your organization wastes when it does somethin that is not 'right first time'. In training and education, th cost of quality includes:

- planning a course for 10 people, but running it fo eight because the time did not suit two people;
- learners starting courses for which they were not ready and dropping out without completing;
- lecturers having to re-mark assignments because th initial marking scheme was not adequately standardized;
- learners failing an assessment because of sub-standard teaching.

156

Overall, the aims of TQM have been summarized as:

- focus on the needs of the market;
- achieve top quality performance in all areas, not just in the product or service;
- establish simple procedures for quality performance;
- continually review processes to eliminate waste;
- develop measures of performance;
- understand the competition and develop a competitive strategy;
- ensure effective communication;
- seek never-ending improvement.

(Adapted from *Total Quality Management* (DTI))

When comparing QA and TQM, I think the most significant difference lies in TQM's addition of cost to the quality debate. QA ignores cost – or money in any form – whereas TQM uses cost as a critical performance measure.

TQM's cost reduction/quality increase aim is summarized by Figure 8.1. It shows how, by spending more on prevention of problems and less on inspection, the amount of waste or reworking can be reduced, resulting in an overall better quality at a lower cost.

TQM – basic principles

Design

TQM places a heavy emphasis, as does QA, on getting the initial design right. Starting with the market, an organization has to be certain that it has identified what the market really wants and then has to translate that into a design specification which is deliverable. It is no use proposing an apparently perfect product or service if it would cost too much to make or the staff skills are not available. For instance, a college might decide that an interactive video was the perfect training medium for an identified need but,

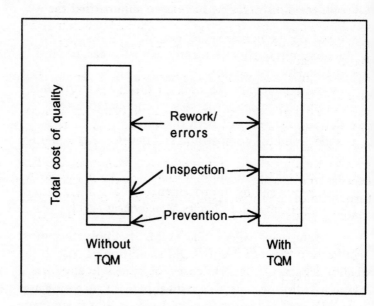

Figure 8.1 *Cost reduction through error prevention*

if the college had no skills in IV, would it be wise to commit itself to delivering the solution?

Within the design stage, TQM also includes the conformance-to-design stage. This involves checking before starting development work that the detailed design still meets the identified need. This stage is comparable to contract review in BS 5750. Checks of this type help to ensure that the development is market focused and to keep down possible later reworking costs.

Prevention

In claiming to reduce costs, TQM relies heavily on the prevention of non-conformance. Typically in manufacturing, 20 per cent of the cost of making a product can arise from reworking. While no figures are available for training and education, it seems reasonable to assume that there is some potential for reducing costs through avoiding the educational equivalent of reworking, such as learners having to repeat a course.

To minimize reworking there needs to be a detailed and on-going analysis of why reworking is needed. Each occurrence is an opportunity to find and eliminate a cause. For example, one group may do badly on a course because they had an inexperienced trainer; another may do badly because the course selection system was faulty; yet another because the learning materials were poorly designed. In turn, each of the three cases would lead to reviewing staff training, student selection and learning materials design.

Continuous monitoring

With the emphasis on prevention of rework rather than the detection of non-compliance, TQM requires a much higher level of monitoring of the production or service process than does QA. This is not monitoring by management, but self-monitoring by the people who carry out the detailed tasks. Invariably the monitoring techniques are designed by the people carrying out the tasks, who see the techniques as helping them to do a good job.

To what extent such techniques can ever be applied to training and education remains to be seen.

TQM – basic methods

Quality circles

The practical application of TQM is based on natural work groups, eg the staff of one department, the staff of the admissions office, or the staff of the canteen. If these groups are large (say, more than 10 people), then they would be sub-divided into smaller groups. These groups are called quality circles, and it is their job to monitor the quality of the work in their area, to identify where quality improvements are needed and to solve quality problems. Such groups are given training in problem solving methods (see below).

Training and education quality circles might work on such problems as:

- the high drop-out rate on course X;
- the low pass rate on course Y;
- why does course A cost 20 per cent more per learner than course B?
- how can we produce OHP acetates which look more attractive?
- what can we do to ensure that a higher proportion of our students find jobs?

Measuring quality

As the above examples show, TQM requires staff to identify a wide range of quality measures. Once identified, staff then monitor the organization's performance on these measures. Since a principle of TQM is that frequent feedback enables staff to improve quality better than infrequent feedback, TQM favours things which can be measured as the process (in this case, teaching) goes along. For example, if your sole measure of the quality of a three-year course is an end of course exam, you will have to wait a long time for the feedback. Indeed, this is itself an ideal quality circle problem: 'Given that we are running a three-year course and need to know now how well we are doing and how we could do better, what measures can we devise?'

An elegant measure used by a School of Nursing involved regularly asking learners how confident they felt about their mastery of the course objectives taught so far. If the confidence measure is plotted against time, a quality measure such as Figure 8.2 results. This allows staff to catch dips such as week 5 and week 10, investigate the cause, and decide on action.

If TQM is ever to apply to training and education, then it

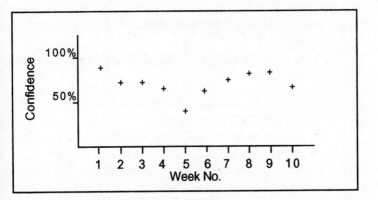

Figure 8.2 *Longitudinal measure on a course*

will only be able to do so because suitable measures of day-to-day or week-to-week performance have been devised. I suspect that the right approach would be to think of the learning group and tutor together as a quality circle and for the group to monitor its own performance with questions such as:

- How would we know if each week's training had been a success?
- Did anything happen last week that could have been done better?
- How can we, the learners, monitor our own progress better?
- How can we, the learners, give better feedback to our tutor on our progress?

Problem solving

TQM places great stress on problem solving within the quality circles. The assumption is that those nearest a problem are likely to find the best solution – but only if they are trained to do so. Formal training in problem solving is therefore an important component of TQM and a

161

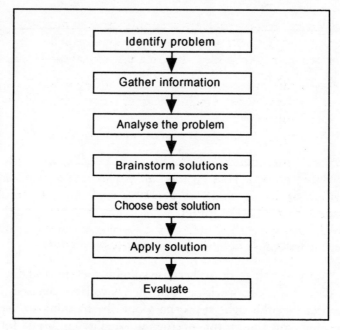

Figure 8.3 *Formal problem solving*

formal algorithm for problem solving is likely to be introduced. Such an algorithm is illustrated in Figure 8.3.

In a manufacturing approach, formal problem solving can be used to help redesign production systems or tools. It can even lead to production workers identifying a design modification that will make the product easier to manufacture. Again, these methods might well work in training and education, either in a quality circle of teachers or in a quality circle of teacher plus learner group. Such a group might tackle a problem like, 'This course does not seem to link the course work very well with our jobs. How could the course be redesigned to improve the link?'

Task groups

The quality circle problem solving activities clearly have to be restricted to problems that are located in the circle's

162

work area. Some problems are multi-area or multi-function, in which case task groups are set up. Problems which such groups might tackle in training and education include:

- co-ordination between marketing and teaching;
- identifying ways of making learner records more accessible to trainers;
- how to spend a special allocation of money.

In one sense, training and education already does this. Working groups, task groups and so on are a familiar method of finding solutions to *ad hoc* problems. Where I suspect that TQM is different is in the frequency with which such groups are used and its very high emphasis on team work rather than departmental rivalry.

Suggestions

Finally, an individual may have an idea for a quality improvement but be in no position to take action. TQM systems always provide for suggestion boxes to trap such ideas. Some companies have reached 40 suggestions per employee per year – a rate that could never have been achieved if those companies did not actively respond to the suggestions.

QA versus TQM

The above brief overview of the ideas and some of the methods of TQM now enables me to make a comparison of the two approaches. First, here is a summary of the key ideas in each case.

QA – *essential features*

QA is basically a management system. Its essential features are:

- a mission statement;

163

STRENGTHS	
QA	TQM
A sound management system	Involves everyone
Gives clear 'what to do' guidelines	Leaves staff free to find their own solution
Strengthens management knowledge and control	Forces management to support staff initiative
Gives tight control of suppliers	Aims to reduce costs
Easy to understand	Standards continuously improved
Sets a standard	Applies to all stages of a process

Table 8.1 *Relative strengths of QA and TQM*

- a set of procedures which lay down how work shall be carried out;
- an auditing system to check compliance to procedures;
- a corrective action system to rectify non-compliance;
- a management review system to monitor and develop the system.

The thinking behind a QA system maintains that:

- quality standards are derived from the customers' requirements;
- once established, if staff work to defined systems, those quality standards will be met;
- while staff help establish standards and write procedures, QA systems are more about compliance than initiative.

TQM – essential features

TQM is essentially a system in which:

164

WEAKNESSES	
QA	**TQM**
Bureaucratic	Highly bottom-up: management have less room to control
Rigid procedures inhibit initiative	Concentrates on short-term measurability
Paper heavy	Meeting heavy
Slow to respond to new needs	
Can focus on the wrong things	
Ignores cost	
Concentrates on interfaces	

Table 8.2 *Relative weaknesses of QA and TQM*

- every employee is enjoined to make continuous efforts towards continuous improvement;
- quality is measured more or less continuously by staff;
- small groups of staff act immediately on any problems which they identify;
- work methods are adjusted daily by small groups of staff in an effort to find ever more cost effective ways of achieving ever increasing quality.

The thinking behind a TQM system maintains that:

- quality standards should be improved all the time;
- once established, a standard is there to be bettered;
- all staff are under an obligation to identify problems and to share in finding solutions.

I now wish to look at the strengths and weaknesses of these two quality philosophies (see Tables 8.1 and 8.2).

165

Conclusions

I do not intend to attempt to draw any firm conclusion as to the merits of QA versus TQM. Indeed, I think that there is too little evidence of the application of either method in training and education to make conclusions valid. What can be said, though, is that training and education cannot expect to escape the current drive towards higher quality and being more answerable to the customer. They will therefore need some means of measuring their performance more sensitively than in the past and some means of improving on past performance. However such a need is phrased, it is pointing towards some form of quality assurance. Perhaps QA will fit the need. Perhaps TQM will. If neither does, we shall have to find some other approach soon.

Appendix 1

PROCEDURE FOR COUNSELLING AND ENROLMENT

VERSION 1

1 PURPOSE

1.1 The purpose of this procedure is to set out how enquirers are to be assisted in making decisions about whether to enrol with the centre.

2 SCOPE

2.1 The procedure shall be followed whenever an individual enquirer approaches the centre by letter, telephone or in person and asks either for details of courses on offer or for advice on a choice of course.

2.2 The procedure shall not be used when an employer or other sponsor approaches the centre about courses on offer. In such cases, the procedure on corporate enrolments shall be used.

3 RESPONSIBILITIES

3.1 Overall responsibility for the admissions system and for the monitoring and revision of this procedure shall lie with the Senior Tutor (Admissions).

3.2 Any person who is requested by the Senior Tutor (Admissions) or by a Head of Department, to offer admissions counselling shall, for the purposes of this procedure, be termed an admissions counsellor.

3.3 Any person who is formally employed in the centre reception office or on the centre switchboard shall, for the purposes of this procedure, be termed a member of the reception staff.

4 DEFINITIONS

Corporate enrolment: a corporate enrolment is one where the enrolment form is signed by the student's employer in the box 'corporate sponsor'.

Quality records: the quality records for this procedure are those items underlined in section 6.

5 REFERENCES

5.1 **Corporate enrolment procedure**: refers to procedure number CEP010 Procedure on handling corporate enrolments.

5.2 **Admissions enquiry form**: refers to Form ADM105 Record of admissions enquiry – see Appendices.

6 PROCEDURE

6.1 Reception staff shall handle initial enquiries, recording their names and addresses and handing (or sending) them a copy of the enrolment pack.

6.2 Reception staff shall offer each enquirer a counselling appointment with an admissions tutor. Such appointments shall be recorded in the counselling diary and assigned to one of the admissions tutors by the reception staff. The assignment shall be recorded in the counselling diary and the admissions tutor concerned shall be notified on form C3 by the reception staff. Admissions tutors must be given 48 hrs notice of appointments.

6.3 The admissions tutor shall counsel the enquirer and record any outcomes agreed with the learner on an admissions enquiry form.

6.4 If, at the counselling session, the learner definitely decides not to enrol, the admissions tutor shall record the reasons given by the learner on the admissions enquiry form.

6.5 If the enquirer completes an enrolment form at the counselling interview, the admissions tutor shall note the course(s) enrolled for on the admissions enquiry form. Completed enrolment forms and admissions enquiry forms shall be passed by the admissions tutor to the registry on the same day as they are completed.

7 APPENDICES

7.1 Admissions enquiry form

[The actual form itself would appear here.]

7.2 Flowchart

[The actual flowchart would appear here.]

Appendix 2

WORK INSTRUCTION No. 123 Edition No. 3

CHECKING A TRAINING ROOM

This work instruction is to be used for checking a centre training room no more than half a working day before a booked training event.

Room No: ......   Date and time of check: ....

Item	Standard Check	Comment
	$\sqrt{}$ or X	
Has trainer specified:		
– table positions?	☐	
– chair positions?	☐	
– A/V requirements?	☐	
Is floor clean?	☐	
Are surfaces dust-free?	☐	
Are tables in specified positions?	☐	
Are chairs in specified positions?	☐	

Is A/V equipment in place?	☐

OHP projector:
- plate and reflector clean? ☐
- bulb working? ☐
- spare bulb present? ☐

Video monitor:
- channel correct? ☐
- picture OK? ☐
- sound OK? ☐

Test video player:
- picture OK? ☐

Video monitor:
- channel correct? n/a ☐
- picture OK? 4 MHz bars
  visible? ☐
- sound OK? n/a ☐

Room locked when check
complete? ☐

Check completed by: ....

On completion this form should be returned to the
training centre administrator.

Bibliography and Addresses

Bibliography

Arter, Dennis R (1989) *Quality audits for improved performance.* ASQC Quality Press, Wisconsin.

BS 4778 Quality vocabulary Part 1: 1987 International terms. BSI.

BS 5750 Part 0: 1987 Principal concepts and application Section 0.1 Guide to selection and use. BSI.

BS 5750 Part 0: 1987 Principal concepts and application Section 0.2 Guide to quality management and quality system elements. BSI.

BS 5750 Part 1: 1987 Specification for design/development, production, installation and servicing. BSI.

BS 5750 Part 2: 1987 Specification for production and installation. BSI.

BS 5750 Part 3: 1987 Specification for final inspection and test. BSI.

BS 5750 Part 4: 1987 Guide to the use of BS 5750. BSI.

BS 5750 Part 8: 1987 Guide to quality management and quality systems elements for services. BSI.

McRobb, Max (1990) *Writing quality manuals for ISO 9000 series.* IFS Publications, Bedford.

Total quality management: A practical approach (nd). DTI.

Zimmerman, Carolyn M and Campbell, John J (1988) *Fundamentals of procedure writing,* Kogan Page, London.

Addresses

BSI
Linford Wood
Milton Keynes MK14 6LE
Tel: 0908 221166

National Accreditation Council for Certification Bodies
  (NACCB)
Second Floor
3 Birdcage Walk
London SW1H 9JH
Tel: 071-222 5374

Index